American History

Discovering America's Lost Stories

Table of Contents

Introduction

History is often perceived through a lens of bias and selective narrative. It is a broad and complex story composed of countless events, personalities, and decisions that shape our present and future. However, many of these episodes remain hidden from the mainstream discourse, rarely making their way into modern textbooks or media. This book seeks to unearth some of these overlooked episodes, providing readers with a fresh perspective on the rich and diverse history of the United States.

The purpose of this book is not merely to recount historical events but also to shine a light on the stories that have been overshadowed by more prominent narratives. From secret societies that influenced the Founding Fathers to the unsung heroes of the Underground Railroad, from the deceptive tactics of the Ghost Army to the valiant resistance of Native American leaders, this collection of stories aims to captivate and educate. Each chapter is a journey into the past, offering a unique glimpse into the events and figures that played crucial roles in shaping the nation yet remain relatively unknown.

What sets *Untold American History* apart from other historical accounts is its focus on the extraordinary and the lesser known. This book does not aim to replace the well-trodden paths of popular history but to complement them with new insights and intriguing tales. By delving into these hidden chapters, readers can gain a more comprehensive understanding of American history, appreciating the complexity and diversity of the experiences that have contributed to the country's development.

One of the greatest benefits of exploring history, especially its less popular facets, is the opportunity to see the world through different eyes. It allows us to question established narratives, challenge our assumptions, and appreciate the multifaceted nature of human experience. This broader perspective is not only intellectually enriching but also fosters a deeper sense of empathy and connection to our shared past.

You will discover a treasure trove of fascinating stories that highlight the resilience, ingenuity, and courage of individuals and groups who have often been forgotten. These narratives provide valuable lessons and insights, reminding us that history is not a monolithic account but a mosaic of diverse voices and experiences. By bringing these stories to light, we can honor the contributions of those who have been marginalized in historical accounts and be inspired to delve deeper into the complexities of the past.

The beauty of this book lies in its ability to cater to a wide range of interests. Whether you are drawn to the mysteries of the lost colony of Roanoke, the bravery of women who tamed the Wild West, the quirks of Emperor Norton, or the peculiar tragedy of the Great Boston Molasses Flood, there is something here for everyone. Each chapter stands on its own, allowing readers to explore the topics that most pique their interest. This flexibility ensures that you can engage with the book in a way that resonates with you, whether that means reading it cover to cover or diving into specific chapters.

Now, let these pages transport you to a different time and place, revealing the hidden depths of the American experience.

Chapter 1 – Secret Societies Unveiled

In the twilight of America's early years, as the nation took its very first steps to grow and develop its identity, there existed a different kind of power—a power that moved unseen, whispering through the corridors of influence. This was the world of secret societies, enigmatic groups shrouded in mystery and shadow, whose influence often extended far beyond the public eye.

It was a time of great change and upheaval. The Revolutionary War had given birth to a new nation and, with it, a new set of ideals and challenges. Amidst this backdrop of uncertainty, secret societies emerged, offering a sense of belonging and purpose to those who sought something more. These societies, often cloaked in rituals and symbolism, promised their members not only camaraderie but also a chance to wield significant influence behind the scenes.

Imagine a dimly lit room hidden away in the attic of a colonial mansion. A group of men dressed in fine but discreet clothing gather around a long oak table. At the head of the table, a figure stands, his face partially obscured by the flickering candlelight. He raises a glass, and the others follow suit, their eyes reflecting reverence and anticipation. This scene is a meeting of the Freemasons, which today is regarded as one of the most well-known secret societies.

With its roots tracing back to the stonemason guilds of medieval Europe, Freemasonry gained popularity in the American colonies rather quickly. Its allure lay in the promise of advancing one's position through a network of influential connections. For many, it was not merely a fraternity but also a pathway to power.

Not surprisingly, among those who were involved in these secretive gatherings were prominent figures of the 18th and 19th centuries. George Washington, Benjamin Franklin, and Paul Revere were some of the names often associated with the Freemasons. Despite already powerful in their own right, they were thought to be drawn to the society's ideals of brotherhood and mutual aid. But of course, putting these noble aspirations aside, their involvement actually had a more pragmatic reason: influence.

However, the Freemasons were not the only controversial society that existed. Some might be familiar with the Order of the Illuminati, while others have heard about the Knights of the Golden Circle. Each of these mysterious societies had its own unique rituals and a hierarchy of members. Some even had secret handshakes. These societies operated in the shadows, with their meetings often held in secluded locations. Their discussions, on the other hand, were often delivered in codes.

The reason men chose to join these societies was multifaceted. Some did so just to feel a sense of exclusivity and the thrill of belonging to a secret and mysterious world. Others, however, sought to secure the benefits that came with membership. They often had their eyes on access to influential contacts, opportunities for political maneuvering, and, of course, the rare ability to shape the course of events the way they wanted without having to step out from the shadows.

Hence, as America grew and blossomed, so did the reach of these secret societies. Their influence could be felt all over the country. From the hall of the Congress to the drafting of the Constitution and the flourishing financial institutions that had taken roots in the new nation. These secret societies were the invisible hands that guided the many levers of power. Apart from the members themselves, only those curious and attentive enough would notice their presence.

Although these societies tried to hold their secrets together, they were definitely not immune to scrutiny. Those curious and attentive enough would never hesitate to go and investigate. Soon, rumors and conspiracies ran wild, painting the societies as puppet masters orchestrating grand schemes. However, rumors are defined as undoubtful truths. Whether tales of these secret societies—or parts of them, at least— hold any truth remains unknown.

While the spotlight of secret societies is often dominated by the Freemasons, let us start our journey by venturing into the less illuminated corridors. The first secret society that we'll discuss is known as the Society of the Cincinnati, founded by officers of the Continental Army, including the one and only George Washington.

The Birth of the Society of the Cincinnati

This particular story takes us to the year 1783. The battle for independence, known to us today as the American Revolution, had raged for eight years, and it was finally over. Although peace was clearly achievable, not everyone was able to sleep soundly. The soldiers and officers who had once marched and fought in countless battles now found themselves at a crossroads. They had a goal during the war, but now their future was uncertain. These soldiers had created a bond, one that those outside of the military would never understand. But even these bonds seemed to fade away after the peace treaty was signed.

The soldiers and officers of war knew they had to do something. It was amidst this episode of uncertainty that one figure voiced out. Gathering in a modest tent near the Hudson River, Major General Henry Know turned to his men whom he had shared the trials of battle with. He knew that their connection must not be lost.

"We must try our best to preserve the ideals we fought for," he firmly addressed the small assembly. "So, let us form a society. One that has the ability to keep our fellowship alive."

And so, the nation witnessed the birth of the Society of the Cincinnati. It was named after a Roman dictator, Lucius Quinctius Cincinnatus, who was known for his victory against the Aequi, a neighboring Italic tribe. Despite having been given the position of dictator, Cincinnatus made a bold decision after the war. He stepped down from his role and returned to the countryside. Here, he tended to his farm and lived a simple life, just as he had done before he was called to fight. His story symbolized the virtues of service and humility that the American army aspired to uphold.

Then, as summer took over, the founding members of the Society of Cincinnati gathered at the Verplanck House in Fishkill, New York. Here, they inked a charter that defined their mission, which was to maintain camaraderie and the ideals of the Revolutionary War. The members of the society had to support one another in times of need.

With their missions made clear, it was time to elect the society's first president. This position went to none other than George Washington. Henry Knox took the mantle as the chief author of the society's constitution.

The Verplanck House, known today as Mount Gulian.[1]

The society had its own insignia, which featured a bald eagle suspended from a blue and white ribbon. This image was chosen as a symbol of their shared service and commitment.

Of course, news of the society's foundation quickly grew. It reached the ears of many officers from across the growing nation. By the first decade, the society welcomed over two thousand officers. However, unlike the infamous Freemasons or even the Hellfire Club (which will be explored later on), the Society of Cincinnati's meetings were usually filled with lively affairs. The members shared stories of past battles with each other and discussed about the future. It was through particular society that

The insignia of the Society of the Cincinnati.[2]

the Revolutionary soldiers were able to keep the spirit of the American Revolution.

Yet, not everyone was fond of the society. Membership requirement was passed down to the eldest male descendants of the society's officers. This hereditary membership led to a storm of controversy, which eventually attracted the attention of several prominent critics, such as Thomas Jefferson and John Adams. Their fear was that the society might turn into an aristocracy, which they thought would sooner or later undermine the principles of equality and democracy they had long fought to establish.

Later on, pamphlets and articles were circulated across the nation, each labeling the Society of the Cincinnati as a threat to the republic. The founding members were left with no choice but to come forward and defend their intentions. They emphasized to the public that the hereditary membership was meant to honor and preserve the memory of their service. They did not want to create a privileged class. The public changed their mind afterward; it was clear that the society posed no threat to their liberty. However, it is almost impossible to suppress rumors entirely. Suspicions still lingered in the air, and debates occurred once in a while.

Although the society had its fair share of critics, it is hard to dismiss its significant contributions, especially when it came to advocacy for veterans' rights. Those who had served in war were often neglected by the government when peace was within reach. This left soldiers and officers in dire straits. The Society of the Cincinnati lobbied for pensions and land grants, ensuring that the veterans could receive the recognition and support they deserved.

Not only did the society bring much-needed attention to the plight of those who had sacrificed so much for their country, but it also managed to forge and strengthen the bonds of brotherhood among veterans and the society's members. To put it simply, the existence of the Society of the Cincinnati provided a lifeline for many, offering both practical help to those in need and a sense of solidarity.

However, not everything is meant to last forever. The society's prominence gradually declined in the early 19th century. By the mid-19th century, its membership had dropped tremendously to fewer than three hundred members, which is a steep drop considering that the society had over two thousand members in the first decade after its establishment.

The Hellfire Club and Benjamin Franklin

It appeared to be just a typical day at the West Wycombe Estate. But one could not say the same about what was happening beneath the estate. In the tunnels under the estate, in the dead of night, there was a group of men walking slowly. They each donned a robe, the kind that was often worn by monks. No words were uttered. These men also wore masks to hide their identity. Walking beside them was a group of women dressed as nuns. One would think this was a scene of religious devotion or a gathering of religious figures. It was actually the opposite; these people were members of the Hellfire Club, a society thought to have been born out of carnal pleasures and rituals performed to mock the very foundations of religious belief.

The Hellfire Club traces back to England. It started with Philip, Duke of Wharton, in 1718. Apart from being a powerful Jacobite politician (a supporter of the deposed James II and his descendants in their quest to reclaim the British throne), the duke of Wharton was also known as a writer and the grand master of the premier Grand Lodge of England (a high position in Freemasonry). He held massive influence and thrived in multiple careers. But the duke had another life behind the scenes. He was not only a notorious drunkard, but he also gained popularity as a rioter, an infidel, and a "rakehell" (a term used to describe a man of immoral habits).

Considering the fact that Philip favored debauchery, perhaps it should not come as a surprise that his Hellfire Club was an exclusive organization for high-society rakes. The reason behind the club's establishment was simple: to shock and ridicule religious beliefs. The members would perform mock religious ceremonies and other activities that were both scandalous and sacrilegious. It has been said that during these mock religious ceremonies, the supposed president of the club could be seen portraying none other than the devil himself.

Luckily, the Hellfire Club was not around for too long; after all, their gatherings were a direct affront to the moral fabric of society. This was largely due to Philip's enemies in Parliament. Driven by political scheming and possibly a desire to see the duke's downfall, members of Parliament directly targeted the Hellfire Club, particularly its immoral activities. A law against horrible wickedness was passed that eventually sparked numerous investigations of the club. Philip faced immense pressure, and he was forced to resign from Parliament. The duke crumbled under the weight of public condemnation. And so, the disbandment of the Hellfire Club was made official.

Of course, this was not the last of the Hellfire Club. In 1746, another figure revived the notorious society.

The man responsible for the rebirth of this scandalous club was Francis Dashwood. Described by many as a charismatic man, Dashwood became one of the wealthiest gentlemen in England thanks to the inheritance left by his father. At the age of only fifteen, Dashwood gained his father's titles, as well as the West Wycombe Estate. With this new fortune, he was able to travel for many years. It is believed that Italy became one of his favorite destinations. He formed a deep interest in the art and culture of classical antiquity. Although Dashwood gained a new set of interests, he also developed a new behavior. Dashwood openly displayed his disdain for religious customs, and his irreverent actions caught the attention of many. Because of this, he was expelled from the Papal States.

Instead of learning his lesson, his anti-religious sentiments grew to the point where he planned on establishing a club for those like himself. Upon his return to England in 1746, Dashwood gathered a group of wealthy pleasure-seekers at the George and Vulture Pub in London, which still operates to this day. These men were the earliest members of Dashwood's Hellfire Club. Initially, the club had a longer name: the Order of the Knights of St. Francis. To maintain the club's discretion, there were few members. Ironically, there were twelve of them, a nod to Christian numerology.

Just like its predecessor, Dashwood's club reveled in satirical anti-Christian activities. Of course, these kinds of activities could not be done in public. So, Dashwood turned to the ruins of Medmenham Abbey. He hired an architect, Nicholas Revett, to help him restore the ruins. Once it was done, Medmenham Abbey was turned into the club's headquarters. The abbey's motto, "Fais ce que tu voudras" ("Do what thou wilt"), encapsulated the club's philosophy of hedonistic freedom. Members of the Hellfire Club would dress in mock religious attire and enjoy a debauched lifestyle. They held banquets, drank alcohol like there was no tomorrow, and performed mock religious ceremonies. Members also allegedly indulged in black magic and satanic rituals. These claims, however, have never been confirmed.

Medmenham Abbey.[3]

Dashwood and his associates soon moved the club's activities to the West Wycombe Caves. This network of manmade caverns was located right beneath Dashwood's estate. One can only imagine what kind of immoral activities and ceremonies were held here. One of the chambers had a wax figure of Dashwood's close friend, the club's secretary, Paul Whitehead. Right beside it was an urn, which many believe to contain Whitehead's heart, which was extracted after his death.

The Hellfire Caves tunnel.[4]

Venturing farther into the network of caves, one would come across the "Great Hall." This beehive-shaped room is easily recognizable with its black marks on the walls that resulted from oil thrown and set on fire during gatherings. This fire was not used for any specific ritual; it acted more like a lamp. Social meetings often took place in this hall. Within this hall was also a set of alcoves. Each of the alcoves once featured beds, all of which were hidden behind little railings with curtains. Beneath these alcoves, one could find linear engravings, which were tally marks of sexual conquests done by each member of the club.

One of the most popular features of the caves is a fake river. It was meant to represent the River Styx from Greek mythology, which separates Earth from the Underworld. Across this river stood the "Inner Temple." This small, circular room was purposely built directly beneath West Wycombe's St. Lawrence Church. Here, directly beneath the church's altar, the members held their most secret and transgressive rituals.

Now, some might wonder what the Hellfire Club has to do with American history. Well, its direct influence on American history is limited, but the depraved club had connections to a Founding Father: Benjamin Franklin.

Franklin was a close friend of Dashwood's and was believed to have attended gatherings of the Hellfire Club during his time in England. However, it is important to note that while Franklin might have been a member of the infamous club, that was pretty much it—there was no branch of the Hellfire Club in the United States. Nevertheless, the club's connection to Benjamin Franklin provides an intriguing and lesser-known link between European intellectual circles and the American Enlightenment. The club's ethos of questioning and challenging established norms echoed the revolutionary ideas that were taking root in the American colonies.

The Hellfire Club declined in the decade after its foundation. It came to an end in the early 1760s. This was possibly due to Dashwood's increasing duties and responsibilities in society. To this day, no one can prove exactly what activities the club performed. No records were ever found, largely due to Paul Whitehead. Before his death, the secretary was said to have ordered the club's records to be burned to ashes. Its activities will forever be shrouded in mystery.

The Mystical Order of Rosicrucianism

Moving on from the eerie Hellfire Club, we'll explore a rather different movement of the early 17th century. Known as Rosicrucianism, this mystical and philosophical movement is linked to Christian Rosenkreuz. However, he is often regarded as a fictional character rather than a historical figure. According to the writings of Johann Valentin Andreae, a Lutheran theologian from the 17th century, Rosenkreuz was said to have been born in 1378 and lived for 106 years.

His legend tells of travels to the Middle East and North Africa in search of esoteric wisdom. After returning to Germany in 1403, he is said to have established the Rosicrucian Order and built a sanctuary in 1409, where he was later entombed upon his death in 1484. The discovery of his tomb 120 years later was purportedly the event that led to the public revelation of the order's existence.

Rosicrucianism came to the surface with the publication of manifestos named *Fama Fraternitatis* and the *Confessio Fraternitatis.* They describe the existence of a secret society of alchemists and sages who were dedicated to the pursuit of hidden knowledge and spiritual truth. It was also through these texts that one could find the principles and goals of the Rosicrucian brotherhood. Since Rosicrucianism blends elements of mysticism, alchemy, hermeticism, and esoteric Christianity, these writings appear to be a call for reformation of science, religion, and society.

Although Rosicrucianism experienced a dramatic decline in the 18th century, it eventually found fertile ground in early America. This was the time when the quest for new knowledge and the pursuit of enlightenment were highly valued. Because of this, the movement's emphasis on wisdom and spiritual transformation found a strong foundation among many American thinkers. They were drawn to the movement's promise of deeper understanding and personal enlightenment. When a general occult revival took place in Europe and the United States sometime in the 19th century, new Rosicrucian societies were born.

The first of these in America was the Rosicrucian Fraternity, established in San Francisco in 1858 by Pascal Beverly Randolph, an American spiritualist and abolitionist. Randolph played an important role in introducing Rosicrucian ideals to the United States. He combined these ideals with his spiritualist practices and progressive social views.

Several other groups emerged out of Freemasonry, such as the Societas Rosicruciana, founded in England in 1866, and the Societas Rosicruciana in Civitatibus Foederatis, established in the United States in 1880. Blending with Masonic traditions, all of these organizations continued to promote Rosicrucian principles.

However, the most successful modern Rosicrucian groups emerged in the 20th century. One of these, the Ancient Mystical Order Rosae Crucis (AMORC), was founded in New York City in 1915 by Harvey Spencer Lewis. Lewis said he had learned the teachings from European Rosicrucians and attracted new members by offering his lessons through the mail. He believed that Egypt was the birthplace of Rosicrucian wisdom and helped fund a well-known Egyptian museum at the group's headquarters in San Jose, California.

The ideals of Rosicrucianism, such as individual change and intellectual freedom, found a receptive audience in America as the new nation struggled to define itself. Early American intellectuals were also drawn to the movement's secrecy because they believed in the idea of an inner circle of enlightened people governing society.

Rosicrucianism's synthesis of mysticism and rationalism reflected the dual nature of the American Enlightenment. It paired a belief in reason and empirical science with an openness to spiritual and metaphysical exploration. This combination of ideas helped develop the intellectual environment of early America, which valued both scientific research and spiritual growth.

The ideals of Rosicrucianism are still promoted today by groups like AMORC and the Rosicrucian Fellowship, which place a strong emphasis on spiritual growth, personal illumination, and the search for hidden wisdom. These contemporary organizations, which aim to uphold and broaden their teachings, provide fellowship, books, and classes to anyone who are curious about life's mysteries and the possibility of human development.

Chapter 2 – The Slave Rebellions That Shook the South

Slave rebellions, more often than not, were born out of desperation and hope. One of the earliest slave uprisings took place in ancient Rome. It involved a figure popularly known as Spartacus.

Spartacus was a Thracian warrior, but he was captured and sold into slavery. Perhaps thanks to his skills as a warrior, Spartacus became a formidable gladiator. He was popular among the Roman citizens, who came to the arena to watch gladiators shed each other's blood. However, Spartacus longed for the open fields of his homeland. He dreamed of the life that had been stolen from him. And so, one night, he began devising a plan and whispered it to his fellow gladiators. Their goal was simple: to escape or die trying.

The rebellion took place in 73 BCE. The nerve-wracking moment came when Spartacus and his men overpowered the guards and fled to Mount Vesuvius—the same volcano that would one day destroy Pompeii. From here, the revolt swelled, as more slaves joined their ranks.

Spartacus's campaign lasted for two years, and it successfully shook the foundations of the Roman Republic. The rebels won battle after battle, and their numbers grew with each victory. However, the Romans were not new to wars and battles. The rebellion was eventually crushed. Even Spartacus himself fell in battle. Although his body was never found, his legacy endured.

American history has similar tales of rebellion. While Spartacus yearned for freedom while he was in the Roman arena, the enslaved in America dreamed of freedom while they were toiling on the plantations. But before diving deeper, it is essential to understand how African slaves were first brought to the American colonies and the horrors they endured.

Their story began in the early 1600s when Europeans shifted their focus to Africa to fulfill their labor needs. Africans were forcibly transported across the Atlantic Ocean as part of the transatlantic slave trade. They suffered terrible conditions. First off, the enslaved, women and children included, were either captured in raids or wars. Once they were brought on the ships, they were chained together and placed into the dark, stifling, cramped holds. One such vessel was the *Brooks*, which was infamous for its horrific conditions.

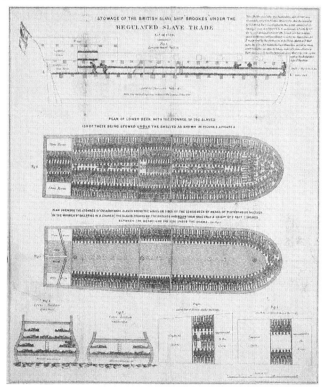

The Brooks slave ship plan.[5]

Unsurprisingly, not all of the enslaved survived the Middle Passage (the journey from Africa to the Americas). Many died due to sickness and the lack of sanitation.

Those who survived were immediately sold at auctions once they arrived in the Americas. Their bodies were thoroughly inspected as if they were nothing but livestock. Slaves who arrived with families were separated, never to see each other again unless by some miracle. They were stripped of their identities and given new names before being subjected to harsh labor.

Life on the plantations was grueling. The enslaved were forced to work from sunrise to sunset. Overseers were everywhere to ensure the slaves never got a second of rest. Those who disobeyed or even made an innocent mistake were given brutal punishments no matter their age and gender. These punishments were not necessarily administered as a lesson; overseers also wanted to instill fear among the enslaved.

Because of that, the methods were designed to torture and belittle them. Whippings, brandings, and mutilations were common punishments. The Derby's dose was likely the most horrific form of torture. Specifically used in Jamaica, this punishment involved forcing the accused slave to lie down. Their mouth was then pried open while another slave was forced to defecate into it. Afterward, the victim was gagged for at least four hours so that they were not able to spit anything out.

Despite the oppression, the spirit of resistance within the enslaved never died. In the late 18th and early 19th century, news of the Haitian Revolution spread like wildfire. Spearheaded by Toussaint L'Ouverture, the massive revolt involved the enslaved Africans in the French colony of Saint-Domingue. The revolution eventually led to the establishment of Haiti as the first Black republic.

This success ignited the flames of resistance among the enslaved on the plantations across the American South. They knew that even in the face of overwhelming odds, the chances of them achieving freedom were possible.

Igbo Landing

The Igbo were well known for their rich traditions and a deep sense of community. They were also known for their resilient nature. Hailing from the southeastern region of Nigeria, enslaved Igbo were initially captured in raids and wars before being forced to travel the Middle Passage. Their destination was often Savannah, where they were to be auctioned off. A plantation owner needed more laborers to work on his estate on St. Simons Island. He purchased the Igbo and loaded the unfortunate slaves onto the schooner *York.*

As the schooner made its way toward St. Simons Island, the Igbo chief made a decision to overthrow their captors and break free from slavery. He whispered his plans to some of his people, who passed the word along to the rest. Waiting for the opportune moment, the Igbo launched their attack. They turned on their captors and overpowered them with the help of the element of surprise. The overseers were definitely caught off guard. Many were quickly subdued and thrown into the water, left to drown.

The schooner drifted and eventually arrived at Dunbar Creek at a site now known as Igbo Landing. However, what happened afterward remains a mystery. There are two main versions. According to one account, after grounding the schooner, the Igbo people walked into the creek together. They sang, "The Water Spirit brought us, the Water Spirit will take us home," in their native Igbo language. Since they believed they were protected by their god, Chukwu, the Igbo chose to die rather than live as slaves. The waters of Dunbar Creek took them, their bodies disappearing as their voices rose in a haunting song. This was their final act of defiance and unity.

There is also another account recorded by an American overseer, Roswell King. According to this version, the Igbo hastily made their way into the swamp right after they landed on St. Simons Island. They chose to die rather than face capture again. Some of them were able to drown themselves before the captors arrived. Those who failed to take their own life were captured and taken to Cannon's Point on St. Simons Island and Sapelo Island. These bounty hunters were said to have been paid $10 for each Igbo slave that they caught.

The area of Igbo Landing.[6]

17

While some believe that Igbo Landing and the surrounding areas are haunted by the souls of the deceased, in African American folklore, the souls of the Igbo are believed to have returned to Africa, carried by the waters of Dunbar Creek.

The Creole Incident

Another lesser-known story of rebellion on the high seas took place aboard the brig *Creole.* The rebellion was led by Madison Washington in 1841. Washington was born into slavery and had already tasted freedom, as he had previously escaped his bonds a year prior to the rebellion. He successfully fled to Canada, but fate had something else in store for him. Washington could not live in peace knowing that his beloved wife, Susan, was still in chains. So, he made the decision to return to Virginia and liberate her. Unfortunately, he was captured again and placed aboard the *Creole.* This time around, he was bound for the slave markets in New Orleans.

The *Creole* carried 135 slaves, of which 103 were from Richmond, Virginia. The remaining thirty-two had been picked up from Hampton Roads, another natural harbor of Virginia. In addition to the enslaved, the vessel also carried tobacco, a crew of ten, and four passengers. This included slave traders, their slaves, and the captain's family.

The slaves were kept in separate holds for men and women. However, unlike the transatlantic slave ships, the captives on the *Creole* were not chained or restrained. Instead, they were locked in the cargo hold.

About a week into the voyage, around half past nine on Sunday, November 7th, the seeds of rebellion began to sprout. The *Creole*'s first mate, Zephaniah Gifford, was on watch when he discovered Washington in the hold reserved for enslaved women. Angered by the sight, Gifford commanded that Washington reveal himself before forcing him to return to his designated spot.

Little did he know, Washington already had a plan in mind. With brute force, he shoved Gifford to the ground. Before Gifford could retaliate, Washington shot him, though the bullet failed to kill him. Washington, with determination burning in his eyes, gathered the others and led the charge against their oppressors.

As the wounded Gifford stumbled to alert the rest of the crew, three other enslaved men, led by Ben Blacksmith, followed and took decisive action. They killed the slave manager, John Hewell, and wounded the ship's captain, Robert Ensor. Ensor and Gifford, realizing the gravity of their situation, attempted to hide from the rebels by climbing the platform atop the mainmast. However, the threat of being shot by Washington forced both Gifford and Ensor to climb down. Washington assured them that they would not be shot if they surrendered peacefully. Blacksmith held a musket to Ensor's chest while Washington demanded that he direct the *Creole* to British territory.

Washington's choice of destination was no accident. He was aware of the British Slavery Abolition Act of 1833, which had outlawed slavery in most parts of the British Empire. The prospect of reaching British territory meant freedom for the captives aboard the *Creole*.

Under duress, Gifford complied, and the *Creole* set a new course for Nassau in The Bahamas. The journey was tense, but the hope of liberty kept the rebels' spirits high. Upon their arrival in Nassau, the British authorities faced a complex situation. The *Creole* incident quickly became a matter of international diplomacy, as American slave traders demanded the return of their "property," while the British were committed to their anti-slavery laws.

The battle for jurisdiction in The Bahamas was fierce. American officials argued that the ship and its human cargo were still subject to US law, while the British maintained that once in their waters, the enslaved individuals were free. The British eventually sided with the captives, setting 128 of the 135 slaves free. The remaining seven were detained on charges of murder related to the rebellion.

In the aftermath of the rebellion, the freed individuals in Nassau faced a new life. Some remained in The Bahamas, integrating into the local communities, while others sought opportunities elsewhere within the British Empire. Madison Washington's fate, like that of many others, is shrouded in mystery, but his act of defiance remains a powerful symbol of resistance.

The Charleston Plot of 1822

The last significant event in this chapter of slave rebellions takes us to Charleston, South Carolina, in 1822, where Denmark Vesey planned one of the most ambitious slave uprisings in American history. He hailed from St. Thomas in the Caribbean, where he had been enslaved his whole life. However, his life changed in 1800 when he won a lottery. With this newfound fortune, Vesey purchased his freedom. He then took up carpentering. Later on, Vesey became a prominent member of the African Methodist Episcopal Church in Charleston.

Like many others who suffered on the plantations, Denmark Vesey was deeply affected by the success of the Haitian Revolution. He dreamed of leading a similar uprising in Charleston, especially when the town had more enslaved Blacks than Whites. Vesey sought to strike a blow against the institution of slavery and secure freedom for the enslaved.

Vesey spent years ensuring the revolt would face minimal obstructions. He recruited trusted enslaved people to his cause and worked to free as many Black men as possible. He even organized secret meetings. The usual meeting place was his home, where he quietly shared his plans. Whenever he saw even the smallest glimpse of fear in the eyes of his followers, Vesey would inspire them with stories of the Haitian Revolution. He envisioned a coordinated attack on Charleston. They would seize the city's arsenals, kill the White inhabitants, and sail to Haiti, where they would be welcomed as heroes.

The rebellion was set to unfold on July 14th, 1822. This was also the same date as Bastille Day; perhaps it was intentionally chosen as a symbolic nod to the French Revolution. After years of meticulous planning, Vesey and his followers were ready to strike. Unfortunately, some had cold feet, and a few nervous recruits chose to betray Vesey. They informed their masters of Vesey's plan a month before the rebellion was supposed to commence. The information quickly traveled to the authorities, who wasted no time in preventing the uprising.

On the night of June 16th, 1822, the city militia rushed to arrest anyone they suspected of being conspirators. Even Vesey himself was captured and brought to trial. Although he maintained his innocence in court, he was pronounced guilty. On July 2nd, 1822, Denmark Vesey and five others were hanged. Thirty-five more were executed, while another thirty-one were exiled.

The rebellion had been foiled before it even started. Still, news of this potential revolt sent shockwaves through the South. The sheer scale of Vesey's plan terrified the White population. As a result, the authorities took extra precautions. New laws were passed to restrain the movement and assembly of Black people. The saddest part is that the African Methodist Episcopal Church, which was once a hub of resistance, was burned and destroyed.

Despite everything, Vesey's name has not been forgotten. He became a symbol of resistance, and his story of martyrdom in the struggle for freedom inspired future abolitionists.

Chapter 3 – The Lost Colony of Roanoke

People have long been captivated by unsolved mysteries. These riddles bridge the gap between the unknown and known by appealing to our deepest sense of wonder.

Despite contemporary technological advancements like carbon-14 dating, several mysteries continue to be unresolved. These riddles are part of the continuous narrative of human curiosity. They serve as a reminder that, despite all of our advancements, there are still mysteries in the world just waiting for us to solve them—or to be left alone.

Take the year 1930 as an example. The vast expanse of the Pacific Ocean became the culprit behind the disappearance of Amelia Earhart. Nearly everyone around the world wonders about her fate. There is also the mystery of the Bermuda Triangle. A few logical explanations have been thrown out by scientists throughout the decades, but there are still some cases that remain unexplainable. There are also unsolved crime cases. Almost everyone has heard of Jack the Ripper, but his identity will likely forever be a mystery.

However, those are not the mysteries that we are about to dissect in this chapter. The lost colony of Roanoke has long intrigued many. The colony began with a man named John White, who initially made a living as an artist and mapmaker. His journey to Roanoke was part of a bigger vision orchestrated by statesman and explorer Sir Walter Raleigh. Having been granted a charter by Queen Elizabeth I, Raleigh set on a quest to explore and colonize new lands in North America.

John White's drawing of the Englishmen's arrival in Virginia.[7]

Of course, the English were driven by many motives. Apart from the promise of new resources and the expansion of their empire, they also wished to establish a foothold that could eventually rival their enemy, the Spanish, who had already built settlements farther south. As for Raleigh, he envisioned a flourishing English presence in the region that would facilitate trade and spread Christianity.

The plan looked simple in the beginning. Roanoke was intended to act as the first step of this ambitious plan. It was supposed to be a base for the further exploration and colonization missions.

John White was tasked to realize this dream. In 1587, he led a group of over a hundred settlers into the Chesapeake Bay area, hoping they could establish a colony somewhere nearby. This location was chosen for a reason. It had deep harbors for larger ships, and it was surrounded by fertile land. Its location was also far from the Spaniards' reach. The rivers attracted the attention of the English too. Waterways were important since they could be a source of food and provide people with better trade and supply routes.

Unfortunately for White and his men, the expedition never reached the Chesapeake Bay. They stopped at Roanoke Island instead, but this decision was initially made to check on the small contingent of men left from a previous expedition. However, upon arriving on the island, they could not spot anyone; their settlement was abandoned, and only bones were found scattered around. What drove their decisions afterward remains unclear, but it appears that their Portuguese navigator, who went by the name Simon Fernandes, insisted on staying on the island. Some suggest he did so because it was getting too late in the season, while others believe there were other navigational and logistical concerns.

The navigator's idea was probably not immediately agreed upon by the settlers, especially since their journey had been filled with challenges from the moment they left the harbor in England. Sailing across the Atlantic had long been a treacherous voyage, and by the time they lowered the anchor at Roanoke, the settlers were already low on supplies. They also had a generous taste of tense encounters with the local Native American tribes. The sudden arrival of the Europeans and the misunderstandings between the tribes and the settlers led the indigenous people to be wary of the English, whose customs were alien to them.

It did not help that John launched an attack against the Native Americans. White had received information from friendly Native Americans about what had happened to the fifteen Englishmen left behind from the previous expedition in 1585. Just as the English suspected, they had been killed. The friendly natives told White that the murders were carried out by warriors from the Secotan, Aquascogoc, and Dasamongueponke tribes. White chose the path of retribution. However, the attack backfired.

Despite having advanced weapons and valuable experience on the battlefield, the settlers were not familiar with the terrain and the ways of the local tribes. They also misidentified their targets. Instead of striking their supposed enemies, the English ended up launching an attack against a group of friendly Native Americans. It is safe to say that the consequences of this decision were immediate and severe. The once friendly tribes, now feeling betrayed and endangered, withdrew their support and assistance.

Without help from the natives, the settlers were left with no choice but to gather supplies on their own. However, this task was not a walk in the park. The harsh coastal environment made the sandy soil unconducive to farming. The summer heat was unforgiving, and the scarce freshwater sources made things difficult. Nevertheless, the settlers worked to build their new community. With the local timber and resources they had on hand, the English constructed the first few buildings: a fort and a series of houses.

John White's responsibilities grew, and his leadership proved crucial, especially during the early days of the new colony. He spent days trying to reestablish relations with the Native Americans. He hoped to secure their cooperation and assistance once again. While many tribes remained hostile, as they viewed the Europeans as invaders, others, like the Croatoan, were more receptive.

The settlers' survival heavily depended on their ability to adapt and persevere. Days turned to months, and the harsh reality of their situation became more apparent. Food shortages were their main threat. Yes, they traded with the Native Americans for food, but it was far from enough to feed every settler.

The inadequate nutrition, harsh living conditions, diseases, and the psychological strain of their isolation tested every ounce of their resilience. However, some remained hopeful and positive. Eleanor Dare (John White's daughter) gave birth to a daughter, Virginia Dare. This newborn was the first English to be born in the New World.

However, as time passed, the settlers' situation grew more dire. The supplies they had brought from England were seriously depleted. They attempted to cultivate the land to no avail, yielding only meager results. The threat of conflict with the Native Americans also loomed large.

The English supply ships were not aware of their whereabouts. Their initial plan had been to settle in the Chesapeake Bay region, but their sudden change of plans caused them to lose contact with the rest. Any hopes of supply ships arriving to save them from starvation were almost nonexistent. Winter was also around the corner, and the settlers knew they had insufficient supplies to see them through the cold, harsh season.

The settlers pressed John White (who was made governor of Roanoke) to set sail to England so that he could return with supplies. At first, he was hesitant to leave his family and everyone else behind. He feared for their safety and survival in his absence. He was also afraid that he would lose his belongings once he left the island. However, after being persuaded—the settlers gave their word to take care of his belongings until his return—White agreed to leave for England. He realized that the urgent need for supplies outweighed his reluctance.

White and his crew eventually reached Smerwick, Ireland, on October 16th, 1587. From here, he was able to make his way to Southampton.

However, two weeks previously, Queen Elizabeth I had issued a general "stay of shipping," preventing any ships from leaving English shores. At this point in time, England was entangled in a conflict with the Spanish Armada. The Spaniards were actually preparing for an invasion. Although White's patron, Sir Walter Raleigh, attempted to provide ships to rescue the colony, the queen overruled this due to the pressing need to defend against the Spanish threat.

In 1588, White was able to scrape together a pair of pinnaces (a type of small, light vessel) for his expedition to Roanoke. These vessels were deemed unfit for military service, so they were not used in the ongoing conflict with Spain. Unfortunately, these vessels were not suited for the Atlantic crossing. White and his crew struggled to cross the ocean. Their misfortune came to a climax when they were suddenly intercepted by French pirates. They were robbed of their supplies, and the journey to Roanoke had to be postponed yet again.

It was only sometime in March 1590 that John White and his crew were able to set sail to the colony. With the threat of the Spanish invasion slowing down, White was able to secure more reliable ships for the journey: the *Hopewell* and *Moonlight*. But, of course, good ships alone were not enough to ensure a smooth sail. White, who had been constantly facing challenges, began to believe that he was cursed by "an unlucky star." He was even more convinced of this when his journey was caught in storms that battered his ships. Navigational errors constantly set them off course, and the death of his mariners to drowning occurred when they reached the Outer Banks.

Finally, on August 18th, 1590, White arrived at Roanoke Island. He was relieved and excited to see his family. It was also the date of his granddaughter Virginia Dare's third birthday. However, his happiness was short-lived. There was no sound coming from the colony. As he got nearer, he noticed that the buildings had all collapsed. White's heart sank. The once-bustling colony he had left only a few years prior appeared to be deserted.

Then, amid the ruins, White's eyes caught sight of a cryptic message: the letters "CRO" carved into a tree and the word "CROATOAN" carved on a post of the fort. Croatoan was the name of a nearby island and a local tribe of Native Americans.

Three years before White left for England, the settlers had agreed to leave a message for him indicating their new location if they ever felt the need to move. However, if the move was done unwillingly or if they had been forced, they were supposed to include an image of a Maltese cross in the message. White scoured the area, looking for an image of the cross. When he found none, White remained hopeful. He tried to think positively; perhaps the settlers, including his family, had moved voluntarily and were still alive.

John White and the settlers discover the abandonment of their colony.[8]

The search for the lost colonists went on. However, the weather soon hampered White's efforts. It became extremely dangerous for the English to continue the search. The captain of the ship demanded that they abandon the investigation. He had lost three anchors already, and losing another was a recipe for disaster. White was reluctant. He still needed to search for his family on nearby islands. Nevertheless, White and his crew returned to Plymouth on October 24th, 1590.

Describing the disappearance of the colony as a tragedy for White is an understatement. Some said he never fully recovered from the loss of his family and the rest of the colonists. Perhaps haunted by the unanswered tragedy, White never returned to the New World. According to his letter sent to the English writer Richard Hakluyt, White expressed his despair but stated there was nothing else that he could do. He left the fate of the settlers and his loved ones to the Almighty.

Over the centuries, the mystery of the lost colony of Roanoke has attracted the public's imagination. Numerous theories emerged. Among the most popular theories is the idea that the settlers had integrated with local Native American tribes, particularly the Croatoan on Hatteras Island. Since they were facing unimaginable hardships and dwindling supplies, the settlers chose to seek refuge with the Croatoan tribe. White discovered the word "CROATOAN" carved into a post and "CRO" etched into a tree. These were the only clues left behind that could hint at the colonists' possible destination.

This theory is further supported by linguistic and cultural evidence that suggests a blending of English and Native American customs. Certain words and phrases in the Algonquian language (spoken by the Croatoan and other tribes in the region) appear to have English origins.

Archaeologist Mark Horton also discovered a few findings on Hatteras Island (sometimes referred to as Site X) that could support this theory. Horton and his team excavated European trade goods, personal items, and tools. A signet ring, gun flints, and pottery fragments were among the items found, which could suggest that there were English settlers on the island. These items also indicate that interaction between the settlers and the Croatoan continued well after the disappearance of the colony.

According to the accounts of later English settlers, these Native American tribes had European features, including lighter skin and blue eyes. These settlers were also astounded when they found out that the natives could speak English and understand English customs. Because of this observation, many began to accept the idea that the Roanoke colonists might have been absorbed into the tribe, their lineage blending over the generations.

Of course, not everyone agrees with the integration theory. Skeptics argue that the European artifacts discovered on Hatteras Island might have been the result of trade rather than direct settlement. They also say that while some Native Americans exhibited European features, these could be attributed to interactions with other European explorers and settlers who came after the Roanoke colonists. Nevertheless, the integration theory is currently the most plausible explanation for the disappearance of the Roanoke settlers.

Another theory revolves around the possibility of Spanish interference. Spain was a dominant colonial power in the Americas during the 16ᵗʰ century. Because of this, the Spanish forces were, more often than not, hostile to English encroachment in the region. A few Spanish records from the period exist that talk about their plans to deal with the English presence in North America. In 1588, the English were sighted in the Chesapeake Bay area by a Spanish expedition led by Vicente González. So, it is plausible that the Spanish might have attacked and decimated the Roanoke colony.

However, archaeological evidence supporting the Spanish interference theory is scarce. There is no direct evidence that could link Spain to the disappearance of the Roanoke colony. Still, the Spanish were known for their ruthless tactics in dealing with perceived threats. Some historians believe that the Spanish could have wiped out the colony and removed any traces that could pinpoint them as the culprits.

Meanwhile, the writings of William Strachey in 1612 tell another story of what happened to the settlers. The English writer and historian wrote an account detailing the early years of another colony known as Jamestown. This account also included a reference to the fate of the Roanoke colonists. According to Strachey, the Roanoke colonists and the Chesepians were slaughtered by the Powhatan tribe shortly before the founding of Jamestown in 1607. He reported that the Powhatan leader, Wahunsenacawh, had been warned by his priests about a prophecy. One day, an unfamiliar nation would arise from the Chesapeake Bay to threaten his tribe. Wahunsenacawh knew he had to stop this prophecy. So, he ordered the massacre of the Roanoke settlers and the Chesepians.

In Strachey's chilling narrative, seven surviving colonists—four men, two boys, and a young woman—managed to escape the slaughter. They chose to make their way up the Chowan River, where they hoped to find refuge. However, the chaos was far from over. The survivors were eventually captured by another tribe. They were then brought to a place called "Ritanoe." They were made prisoners and forced to beat copper.

Although Strachey's account dates back to the 1600s, his theory gained significant acceptance during the mid- to late 20ᵗʰ century. His account fit neatly into the broader narrative of the tumultuous relationships between the Europeans and the Native American tribes. However, it could also be possible that Strachey was biased against

Wahunsenacawh. Modern historians argue that his writings were heavily influenced by the colonial politics and conflicts of his era. It is entirely possible that his account might have been exaggerated.

Apart from these theories and writings, the search for the popular "Dare Stones" in the 1930s added another layer of intrigue to the mystery. The Dare Stones were said to have been discovered by a Californian tourist named Louis E. Hammond in 1937. He claimed he came across the first stone while he was driving through the southeastern United States. According to the tourist, the stone was located near the Chowan River in North Carolina, which was relatively close to Roanoke Island.

Interestingly, the stone had an inscription. It is thought to have been written by Eleanor Dare, who detailed the deaths of her husband and child at the hands of so-called "savages." Part of the inscription reads, "Ananias Dare & Virginia Went Hence Unto Heaven 1591."

A depiction of the first Dare Stone.[9]

Interestingly, Hammond disappeared without a trace after he handed the stone to scholars. The stone was brought to Emory University in Atlanta, where assessments were conducted that confirmed the stone's authenticity. The artifact was from the late 16th century. A frenzy of interest ensued following the news of this potential breakthrough. Rewards were even offered for new stones.

More stones were discovered, each providing more details of the settles' fate. Some included inscriptions of their struggles, another talked about the death of several colonists, and some had messages directed at John White, urging him to rescue them.

However, as the number of stones increased, so did skepticism. Scholars began to note discrepancies in the language and phrases carved on the stones. Many did not align with the English language used in the late 16th century. They contained modern idiomatic expressions that were definitely not used during the Elizabethan era. Furthermore, the later stones appeared more detailed than the first, which raised doubts about their authenticity.

Investigations took place, and authorities looked into the backgrounds of the individuals who claim to have found the stones. Eventually, all but the original Dare Stone was deemed to be forgeries.

The unsolved mystery of the Roanoke colonists has inspired numerous books, documentaries, and theories. Despite happening in the 17th century, recent research efforts have reignited interest in the mystery. With more advanced technologies to uncover new evidence, professionals are still hoping they can shed some light on what happened to the settlers.

Chapter 4 – The Underground Railroad's Unsung Heroes

Despite its name, the Underground Railroad was neither a railroad nor underground. It was a secret network of hidden routes and safehouses established to aid the enslaved in their quest for freedom. Although this complex system began to be widely used by the enslaved in the early 19th century, its roots can be traced back to the late 18th century.

Believe it or not, the Underground Railroad was not a singular organization but a loose coalition of individuals and abolitionists united by the common goal of undermining the institution of slavery. This included free African Americans, White allies, and members of religious groups, such as the Quakers. These people were known as "conductors," and their homes and businesses that served as safe havens were referred to as "stations."

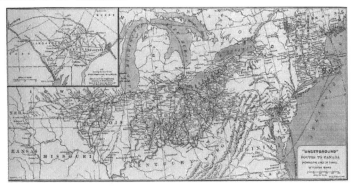

The map of the Underground Railroad to Canada.[10]

This network provided the enslaved with an opportunity to escape from the oppressive conditions of the South and seek a safe haven in the North or Canada, where slavery was prohibited. The secret routes of the Underground Railroad passed through various states. Major stations were located in Philadelphia, Cincinnati, and Detroit, to name a few.

However, the success of the Underground Railroad would not have been possible without several key figures. They were willing to risk their lives to assist the enslaved. One of the most remarkable individuals in this network was Laura Haviland.

Laura Haviland, a Key Conductor of the Underground Railroad

Laura Smith Haviland was born on December 20th, 1808, in Kitley, Ontario, Canada, to Daniel and Sene Smith. Having devout Quakers as parents, it was only normal that Laura was raised in a deeply religious environment. Equality and justice were the main aspects of their beliefs. When Laura was still a child, the Smith family moved to Lockport, New York. Here, they joined a community of other Quaker families. Laura received an education—the Quakers emphasized the importance of education for all, including women— and was taught about the Quaker principles of simplicity and peace.

A portrait of Laura Haviland.[ii]

For those who are not familiar with the Quakers, they were known for their progressive views and practices. Formally known as the Religious Society of Friends, they were ahead of many societal norms of the time. They strongly believed in the inherent equality of all people, no matter their race, gender, or even social status. This idea was founded on the notion that there is "that of God in everyone," which gives each person inherent worth and dignity.

Quakers were also pacifists who advocated for nonviolence and peaceful conflict resolution. Their meetings were marked by silent worship, although any member was free to speak if they were moved by the Holy Spirit. This practice expressed their conviction in having a direct, personal experience with God.

Laura was a highly educated woman. She read extensively and loved the works of John Woolman, a Quaker abolitionist. His accounts of slavery were one of the many things that shaped Laura's cause in helping the enslaved.

In the 1820s, Laura and her family, along with the Havilands—her future in-laws—moved to Adrian, Michigan. Here, she married Charles Haviland, another Quaker who shared her abolitionist sentiments.

The progressive Chandler family also called Adrian home. This family was actively involved in the fight against slavery. Their views and active participation in the abolitionist cause undoubtedly influenced Laura.

Soon, Laura and Charles Haviland's house was turned into a center of anti-slavery activities. In 1837, they established the Raisin Institute, an integrated school that opened its doors to both Black and White students—a concept deemed revolutionary at that time. Apart from providing education, the institute also served as a safe haven for runaway slaves, making it part of the Underground Railroad.

Unfortunately, tragedy struck the Haviland family. In the early 1840s, a severe bacterial infection known as erysipelas began to rise. It infected Laura's family, as well as her friends and neighbors. The infection eventually claimed the lives of Laura's parents, her husband Charles, and even their young daughter. Nevertheless, this massive personal loss did not hamper Laura's commitment to the abolitionist cause. It actually seemed as if the tragedy strengthened her resolve.

Moving forward, her involvement in the Underground Railroad grew even more intense. Laura often traveled under cover of night in disguise to escort the enslaved to safety. Her home and the Raisin Institute remained major stations on the Underground Railroad. She and her allies provided not only shelter but also food and guidance to dozens of fugitives.

Perhaps one of the most memorable episodes in Laura Haviland's life was when she went on a mission to free the children of two fugitive slaves. Willis and Elsie Hamilton had just successfully escaped to Canada, but their children were still trapped in bondage in the South. Their daring escape was discovered by their former master, known as Mr. Chester. Enraged by the escape, he ordered slave catchers to capture them. Fortunately for Willis and Elsie, this plan failed. So,

Chester resorted to deception. He promised that the two would be treated as freedmen if they returned willingly. Chester even said that they would get a chance to be reunited with their children.

Laura knew she had to intervene. Determined to thwart Chester's plan, she set out for Tennessee, accompanied by her son Daniel and a brave student from the Raisin Institute named James Martin, who posed as Willis Hamilton. Upon their arrival, Chester quickly became enraged when he realized that Willis Hamilton was not among the group. In a fit of fury, he held Laura, Daniel, and James at gunpoint, threatening to murder them and kidnap James to enslave in place of Willis Hamilton. However, this was not Laura's first rodeo. She remained calm despite the threat and made use of her quick-thinking skills.

Laura was able to defuse the situation just enough for them to escape from Chester's clutches. But Chester's wrath did not stop there. For the next fifteen years, Chester and his family relentlessly pursued Laura, both legally and through private slave catchers. They sent her a ton of derogatory letters, hoping their threats and nasty words could scare her away from her abolitionist pursuits.

When the Fugitive Slave Law was passed, the Chesters sharpened their knives and built a legal case against Laura. They accused her of not only aiding but also stealing their slaves. Since the law stipulated severe penalties for anyone who helped fugitive slaves, Laura was in grave danger. But luck favored Laura, as the case was brought before Judge Wilkins. The judge's sympathy for the abolitionist movement was a major factor in Laura's evasion of legal repercussions. And so, despite the increasing pressure and legal threats, she managed to avoid conviction.

As one would expect, the legal fights only strengthened Laura's determination in her cause. Seeing as her influence had grown tremendously, she made use of this with both her voice and a pen. She participated in a number of rallies, often giving speeches, and wrote many articles that detailed the evils of slavery. Many were moved by her passion, and these people decided to join the cause.

Her efforts intensified after the Civil War started. During this time of chaos, she worked as a nurse. While tending to the wounded, Laura took the opportunity to continue her advocacy for the emancipation of slaves.

In 1865, the Raisin Institute was purchased by the Freedmen's Aid Commission. It was transformed into the Haviland Home for Orphans. During the Civil War, the Freedmen's Aid Commission was established to help freed slaves and their families make the transition to freedom by offering essential services, including housing, work assistance, and education. Children who had lost their parents, frequently as a result of the violence and unrest of the time, found refuge in this orphanage.

Laura continued her social reforms into her later years. She championed women's rights, prison reform, and temperance. Despite her old age, she remained devoted to making the lives of everyone around her better. Laura also authored her own autobiography, *A Woman's Life Work: Labors and Experiences*. In this book, she shared her experiences and imparted lessons she had learned from a life committed to equality and justice.

Laura Haviland passed away on April 20th, 1898, in Grand Rapids, Michigan, at the age of eighty-nine. Although her name may not be widely known, and her efforts are often overshadowed by those of more well-known abolitionists, her legacy endures.

Jermain Loguen, the Selfless Hero of the Underground Railroad

Another unsung hero of the abolitionist movement was Jermain Wesley Loguen. He was an escaped slave who became an influential abolitionist in Syracuse, New York. The son of an enslaved woman named Cherry and her Irish enslaver, David Logue, Jermain experienced the brutal realities of slavery firsthand.

In 1834, at the age of twenty-one, Jermain escaped to freedom. He did so with the help of a forged pass and the assistance of sympathetic individuals he met along the way. His journey north eventually brought him to New York. Here, he changed his name to Jermain Wesley Loguen, adding an "n" to his surname—a symbolic break from his harrowing past.

A photo of Jermain Loguen from an 1859 autobiography.[12]

Loguen took the chance to further his education in New York. He got married and started a family. In 1841, Loguen and his small family moved to Syracuse. Here, he kept up his enthusiasm for social justice and education. Loguen devoted his life to the abolitionist movement, collaborating with notable leaders like Frederick Douglass. His impressive oratory skills quickly garnered attention, especially when he drew on his personal experiences. His voice became a powerful tool in the fight against slavery.

Loguen was a very confident person. He never shied away from publicizing his work. He boldly placed letters in the Syracuse press detailing his activities and requesting donations to aid freedom seekers. Loguen also encouraged others who were moved by their cause to challenge unjust laws.

A month after the Fugitive Slave Act was enacted, Loguen convinced his adopted hometown of Syracuse to declare itself a refuge for escaped slaves. His proposition was put to a vote and approved by a resounding majority of 395 to 96.

Loguen constructed apartments on his property to serve as hiding places and temporary lodging for escaping slaves. Even his home was turned into a station on the Underground Railroad. Both he and his wife, Caroline, were some of the most active agents in the Underground Railroad network.

The Jerry Rescue incident that took place in 1851 is considered one of the most famous events involving Loguen. William Henry, known as Jerry, was an escaped slave who resided in Syracuse. Things went down when Jerry was arrested by federal marshals acting under the Fugitive Slave Act. Of course, the abolitionist community was enraged by this. Spearheaded by Loguen himself, Jerry was freed when a mob of abolitionists stormed the jail.

Worried for Jerry's safety, Loguen and other abolitionists were said to have hidden him in various locations throughout the city, allowing Jerry to evade recapture. Jerry was eventually transported to Canada, where he was able to live in peace.

Much like Laura Haviland, Jermain Loguen fought for equality in his later years. For years, he used his oratory skills to advocate for the rights of African Americans. Loguen also focused on his religious work, becoming a licensed preacher of the African Methodist Episcopal Zion Church and later a bishop of the same church.

Loguen eventually passed away on September 30th, 1872, at the age of fifty-nine. Many believed that he died due to tuberculosis.

John P. Parker, an Inventor by Day and a Savior by Night

John P. Parker had an almost similar family background to Jermain Loguen. Born into slavery around 1827, Parker had a White father (who was also an aristocrat) and an enslaved woman as a mother. When he was only eight years old, Parker was sold and taken to Richmon, Virginia, before being sold again six months later. This time, he was taken to Mobile, Alabama, where he served as a house servant to a doctor.

The doctor's sons took an interest in Parker's education. The two chose to defy Alabama's strict laws against educating slaves. They often smuggled books from their father's library and gave them to Parker. In the dead of night, the doctor's sons secretly taught Parker how to read and write. Parker devoured every book he could get his hands on. He soon developed a deep interest in literature and loved the works of Shakespeare and other popular English poets of that era.

Parker no longer served as a house servant in the early 1840s. Instead, he was made an apprentice in the iron molding trade. He was quick to master the craft, but his outspoken nature often caused him trouble; it was common for Parker to clash with the foremen, which resulted in his dismissal from several foundries.

The dismissals disappointed the doctor. He made the decision to sell Parker as a farm laborer. However, Parker had other plans. He turned to Elizabeth Ryder, one of the doctor's patients. After persuading her to buy him, Ryder allowed Parker to earn and save his wages to purchase his freedom, which he successfully did in 1845. After buying his liberty, he moved to Indiana before making another move to Cincinnati. He finally ended up in Ripley, Ohio.

John P. Parker's restored house in Ripley, Ohio.[13]

In Ripley, Parker's life began to change. He established a foundry named Phoenix Foundry, which he ran during the day with ten other workers. At night, Parker had another job. He was a conductor on the Underground Railroad. His after-hours shift was usually filled with guiding runaway slaves across the treacherous Ohio River. One time, his rescues required him to sneak into a plantation so that he could save a baby.

The baby was being held hostage by the owner of a plantation to prevent the parents from escaping. Parker started his mission late at night under cover of darkness when all was silent. At this hour, everyone on the plantation was in a deep slumber, allowing Parker to scale the outer walls and slip through the partially open window. He was cautious when stepping on the floorboards; one wrong move could make a creaking sound and wake anyone nearby. Guided by the faint whimpers of the baby, Parker tiptoed down the hallways.

He eventually reached the nursery, where the baby was lying in a crib. He cradled the baby in his arms, holding him close against his chest while retracing his steps. He quickly yet quietly slipped out the window and into the night with the baby safe in his arms. After crossing the Ohio

River, he successfully reunited the baby with the parents, who were overjoyed.

Of course, the more he became involved with the Underground Railroad, the more serious danger he was in. By the 1850s, the Kentucky authorities had placed a bounty of $1,000 on Parker's head. As rumors of his role spread around and investigations began, Parker knew he had to save himself. He publicly denied any participation in the Underground Railroad prior to 1865.

However, his life story was eventually revealed in 1886. The manuscript remained unpublished in the Duke University Archives until 1996, when historian Stuart Sprague brought it to public attention with the publication of *His Promised Land: The Autobiography of John P. Parker, Former Slave and Conductor on the Underground Railroad*.

Parker dedicated his life to his foundry after the Civil War. By 1870, he was regarded as one of the wealthiest individuals in Ripley. He even owned an extensive collection of books. His inventive talent thrived in the 1880s; he received patents for an improved tobacco press in 1884 and a portable version in 1885. He also earned a patent for a soil pulverizer in 1890. Parker became involved in the flour milling business, displaying his products at the New Orleans Exposition in 1884.

John P. Parker passed away on January 30th, 1900.

Chapter 5 – The Ghost Army of World War II

Deception has always been a critical strategy, especially in the theater of war. Centuries ago, war commanders used the art of misdirection, feints, and subterfuge to gain the upper hand. One of the earliest known examples of such tactics happened in the ancient Trojan War, at least according to legend. It seemed as if the siege of Troy would never end. So, the Greeks built a massive wooden horse and hid a force of men inside it. Then, they pretended to sail away. The Trojans, seeing the ships leaving the harbor, believed they had won the war. They brought the wooden horse within their walls as a trophy. Under cover of night, the hidden Greek soldiers emerged and opened the gates for their returning army. Troy fell.

Fast forward to the 20th century, and the world was engulfed in the most devastating conflict in history: World War II. The stakes were higher than ever, and the need for innovative deception strategies became increasingly important.

The Axis and the Allied powers were the key players in this worldwide struggle. On the Axis side were the Germans, commanded by none other than Adolf Hitler. He demonstrated a remarkable skill at strategic deception. One of the most striking examples occurred during Operation Barbarossa. This was the code name for the German invasion of the Soviet Union in 1941.

Hitler and his generals understood that surprising the Soviet Union was critical to the success of their campaign. So, in the months before the invasion took place, the Germans engaged in a few diplomatic tactics that were designed to deceive the Soviets. They even signed a non-aggression pact with the Soviet Union. This led Stalin to believe that Germany had no urgent plant for an eastern offensive. The Germans organized bogus force concentrations in the Balkans and Norway, complete with phantom tanks and planes, to distract the Soviets' attention.

Every effort was taken to maintain the illusion of normalcy, especially when German forces gathered near the Soviet border. Radio silence was imposed, and the Germans broadcasted misleading radio traffic from locations far from the actual assembly areas. They purposely expanded reconnaissance flights over Soviet territory until they became routine enough that no one was suspicious.

It is safe to assume that the Soviet Union was unprepared for the invasion when it finally broke out on June 22nd, 1941. The German advance was staggering in both its scope and speed. Much of the early success of Operation Barbarossa can be attributed to the efficiency of the earlier deception campaigns, though the operation ultimately failed.

Three years went by, and the war in Europe had reached a critical stage. The Allies were planning major liberation operations, including the historic D-Day invasion of Normandy. Gaining a substantial foothold in western Europe would enable the Allies to conduct more operations aimed at pushing the Germans back. Normandy was chosen specifically for its strategic significance. Normandy had a great balance of defensible terrain and access to important highways and ports, which were necessary for supporting the invasion force.

The lessons of deception the Allies had learned from throughout the years were not forgotten. The Germans had a track record for achieving notable successes using their various deceptive tactics.

Colonel Billy Harris and Major Ralph Ingersoll were the masterminds behind the Ghost Army. Harris brought his technical expertise as an engineer to the table. Ingersoll contributed his creative vision and understanding of the psychological aspects of deception. He was a writer and journalist before the war broke out.

The creation of this unit was partly inspired by the British units in Operation Bertram. In this particular episode, the British successfully gained the upper hand during the Second Battle of El Alamein, which took place in Egypt in 1942. The British achieved success through a combination of logistical deception and the use of dummy equipment and camouflage. They also implemented radio deception to conceal their real intentions from the enemy.

Thus, the Ghost Army was born. Officially named the 23rd Headquarters Special Troops, the task of this rather unique unit seemed straightforward; its men were to employ a variety of deceptive techniques to mislead the enemy. However, meticulous planning was needed in order for the deceptions to work.

The Ghost Army later became an important unit in the Allied strategy, including during Operation Bodyguard. The plan was to divert the Germans' attention and protect the Allies' plans for the Normandy invasion. To ensure these deception tactics worked, a diverse group of individuals were recruited into the Ghost Army. Many of them were artists, designers, and engineers. Their skills were invaluable for creating convincing visual and auditory illusions to confuse the enemy.

The Ghost Army's operations revolved around techniques that created the illusion of large military formations. One of their most used and ingenious tactics was the deployment of inflatable tanks and artillery. Since these decoys were made of rubber, they were lightweight and portable. They could be quickly inflated and moved to imitate intimidating armored units.

Sergeant Bill Blass played a big role in this. Making use of his background in art and design—he would later become a renowned fashion designer—he worked to ensure that every inflatable decoy looked as realistic as possible. Perhaps thanks to the sergeant, in the eyes of the enemy reconnaissance planes flying overhead, these inflatables looked absolutely real and minutes away from engaging in battle.

However, visual deception alone would not be enough to fool the enemy, especially one that had an extensive experience on the battlefield. The Ghost Army had to create an immersive experience that would take away any doubts in the minds of German observers. The unit also placed and strategically hid massive speakers on the field that broadcasted the real sounds of tanks rumbling, trucks rolling in, soldiers marching, and generals shouting commands.

An inflatable tank modeled after the M4 Sherman.[14]

The Ghost Army also perfected the deceitful art of fake radio transmissions, better known as "spoofing." Skilled radio operators used carefully designed scripts to send out messages that imitated real-world military communication patterns. These forged messages were intended to be intercepted by the Germans and fed them inaccurate information about Allied military movements and preparations.

Secrecy was taken seriously. Confidentiality about their methods and operations was crucial; not a single word about these operations could be uttered among those outside of the unit. After all, the success of their deception hinged on the Germans believing that the dummy units were real. Anecdotes from members of the Ghost Army highlight the extent they took to conceal their operations. Once, a local farmer stumbled upon an inflatable tank on the field. Not taking any risks, soldiers of the unit had to quickly explain that it was nothing more than a training exercise for the military. The farmer was then sworn to secrecy.

Nevertheless, the Ghost Army faced challenges. Apart from secrecy, speed was one of the most crucial elements. Thorough preparation and coordination were required for the setup and upkeep of the radio transmissions, sound equipment, and inflatable decoys. Oftentimes, soldiers had to work extremely fast and efficiently at night. They had to be ready at all times to quickly assemble and dismantle the decoys before relocating to another assigned field.

However, the Ghost Army's achievements in the war were astounding. The unit's first major mission took place in the days leading up to D-Day. As part of the broader Operation Fortitude, the Ghost Army had to convince the Germans that the main invasion force was going to land at Pas de Calais, not Normandy. This task comprised a number of elaborate deceptions, one of which was the establishment of the First US Army Group (FUSAG) under General George Patton. The Ghost Army succeeded in maintaining this illusion. The Germans believed the real invasion was still to come, although the Allied forces had already stormed the beaches of Normandy on June 6th, 1944. The success of the D-Day invasion marked a turning point in the war.

Operation Brest

Another one of the Ghost Army's feats happened in the late summer of 1944. At this point in time, the Allied forces were making significant advances in France. They had their eyes on the port city of Brest, which was known for its strategic position and supply potential. The Allies knew they had to capture the city, but there was one problem: the Germans had fortified the city. Attacking Brest head-on was completely out of the question, as it would only lead to much bloodshed and a waste of supplies. The Allies had to divert the Germans' attention first before they could make a move. The Ghost Army was needed again.

The unit set up their inflatable tanks, artillery, and vehicles on a field located several miles away from the port city. From a distance, these inflatables, combined with the faint sound of the soldiers' constant movements, appeared real. It was made even more believable when Major Ralph Ingersoll, Sergeant Bill Blass, and Colonel Billy Harris led the efforts on the ground. Fake messages carrying discussions of supply lines and troop movements were created so the Germans would believe an attack on Brest was about to take place at any moment if they intercepted them.

Then, when night came, soldiers of the Ghost Army moved swiftly to move the inflatable tanks into new positions to simulate the tactical adjustments of a real army. Blass and his team worked to ensure that they did not miss a single detail, from the perfectly painted insignias on the decoys to the fake tracks in the mud and the sounds of heavy vehicles moving.

Because of their meticulous planning, the Germans took the bait. They believed that a major assault was to be launched from the Ghost

Army's position. The Germans diverted their forces to counter the perceived attack. With the Germans' attention elsewhere, the real Allied units wasted no time in advancing toward their objectives. They faced less resistance than they would have, which contributed to their successful capture of Brest.

Operation Viersen

Early in 1945, the unit was called upon once again. This time around, the Allies were pushing into Germany and needed a diversion along the Rhine River near the town of Viersen. The Ghost Army was to confuse the Germans by misleading them about the location of the Allied crossing. If this succeeded, the Allies could establish a bridgehead while facing minimal opposition.

Time was of the essence. So, the Ghost Army kicked off their mission with a detailed reconnaissance. They needed to first understand the terrain and observe the typical German patrol patterns to make their deception work. Once again, they placed their inflatable tanks and artillery, along with other props, on their selected field, which was located several miles from the actual crossing point. They also ensured that their location was visible to German reconnaissance planes yet impossible for the enemy to approach head-on.

The Ghost Army positioned mock landing craft along the riverbank, complete with fake soldiers manning them. These acted as an illusion that suggested an imminent river crossing. The noise of engines, water splashing, and soldiers shouting were played through hidden speakers to make the scene even more believable. At the same time, Ingersoll's radio team broadcasted scripted messages that requested additional supplies. These messages even included discussions about crossings and fake reports of scouting missions.

It all went down just before dawn. The German scouts noticed the movement of their enemy's tanks and artillery. Without realizing it was a deception, they reported that a major crossing at the Ghost Army's location was about to take place. Seizing the opportunity, the real Allied forces made their move. They crossed the Rhine River without suffering heavy casualties.

The Disbandment of the Ghost Army

On May 8th, 1945, Germany surrendered. The Ghost Army was one of the many key players in the victory. However, with the arrival of peace, there came a shift in priorities. There was no need for a specialized deception unit anymore. On September 15ᵗʰ, 1945, the special unit was officially disbanded. Although its members were allowed to return to their civilian lives and reunite with their families, their wartime contributions went largely unrecognized.

However, there was a reason for this. For decades, the existence and even the activities of the Ghost Army were kept in a file labeled "classified." Not even the soldiers could discuss or reminisce about their experiences. While the world moved on, the intriguing story of the Ghost Army remained in the darkness, hidden from the public.

It was not until many years later that people heard about the unit for the first time. In the 1980s, the classified records were gradually declassified. The feats of the Ghost Army began to be recognized. Veterans of the once-classified unit—many of whom had gone on to have careers in other fields—could now share their stories and challenges they faced back when they were in service. Medals were designed and presented to show gratitude for the unit's massive contributions in the war.

As more details of the unit were unveiled, public interest grew tremendously. Directors wasted no time in producing documentaries detailing the Ghost Army's strategies, and authors worked day and night, interviewing members of the unit and writing about their experiences.

The Ghost Army medal.[15]

The publication of Rick Beyer's book, *The Ghost Army of World War II*, captured readers' attention with its detailed descriptions of the unit's operations and the stories of the people who made it all possible. This particular book, along with other forms of media discussing the unit, showcased the strategic brilliance of the Ghost Army, helping to ensure that its legacy would never be forgotten.

Chapter 6 – The Rise and Fall of Emperor Norton

The number of times the word "emperor" appears in history books is too numerous to count. From the mighty rulers of ancient Rome who controlled Europe and beyond to the illustrious dynasties of China, where emperors were referred to as the Sons of Heaven, this title has held significant weight. Augustus Caesar, for example, is known for transforming the Roman Republic into an empire, though he never formally accepted the title emperor. Meanwhile, Qin Shi Huang became the first emperor of China after unifying the warring states.

However, as the years went by, the concept of an emperor evolved. These days, it is a more symbolic title. The idea of being an emperor or the ruler above all remains a fascinating concept.

The Life of Joshua Norton Before Rising as the Emperor

San Francisco is a name that many are familiar with. The city is popular for its bohemian spirit and cultural diversity. The city blossomed during the Gold Rush and never stopped developing; it is now a bustling metropolis full of locals and tourists.

In the broader perspective of the United States, a country that prides itself on democracy, the concept of an emperor living in California is strange. Yet, San Francisco once welcomed a man who proclaimed himself emperor. Known as Emperor Norton, he stands as one of the most unique yet lesser-known figures in American history.

He was born Joshua Abraham Norton, but little is known about his early life—a mystery that befits his later eccentricity. His birthplace was England, yet he spent a huge chunk of his youth in South Africa, thanks to the British Empire's colonization programs, which were created to expand British influence across the world. Norton's family was believed to have been involved in trade. They benefited from the economic opportunities that British colonial rule provided.

Norton turned thirty years old around 1849. Sometime during this year, he arrived in San Francisco. While many others arrived in California with nothing more than dreams of benefiting from the Gold Rush, Norton arrived with approximately $40,000. This amount was substantial for the time; it would have been equivalent to over a million dollars today. Norton had everything he needed to start a life in a new place.

Ever the business man, Norton knew he had to take advantage of the city's rapid growth. San Francisco was a magnet for various individuals across the globe. The city was ripe with both opportunities and risks. Norton chose to invest his capital in real estate and the import brokerage business. Perhaps due to his early experiences in South Africa, Norton was able to successfully navigate the volatile market conditions of the time and gradually built a name for himself.

In just less than four years after his arrival in San Francisco, Norton managed to amass a generous fortune. At this point in time, he was worth at least a quarter of a million dollars (equivalent to about $8.7 million today). His success in the real estate market and his ventures in importing goods turned him into one of the city's prominent businessmen.

However, life is not without its challenges. A string of events altered his fortunes. In 1852, China faced a severe famine, which led to a ban on the export of rice to ensure enough food for its own population. The global market was rocked by this. San Francisco was home to many Chinese laborers who relied on rice. When the price of rice began to skyrocket, many were upset. They had to pay thirty-six cents per pound for rice; that would be equivalent to spending almost ten dollars per pound today.

Unsurprisingly, Norton saw a window of opportunity in this crisis. He anticipated that the city's expanding Asian population would continue to have a high demand for rice. He decided to act quickly. He invested twenty-five thousand dollars in a shipment of rice from Peru, purchasing it at twelve cents per pound. His strategy was simple: corner the local market and take advantage of the high prices to generate a massive profit for himself. He was determined that this could double or even triple his investment value.

Well, that didn't happen. His hopes were crushed the moment he learned that his shipment was not the only one on its way from Peru. As he awaited the arrival of his rice, two more ships laden with rice entered the port of San Francisco. This sudden influx of rice overwhelmed the market, causing prices to drop. The price of rice dropped back to three cents per pound, which was a fraction of what Norton paid.

Perhaps consumed by desperation, Norton took the matter to court. He engaged in a legal battle with the vendor who sold him the shipment. Not only did he claim that he was misled about the exclusivity of the deal, but he also sought compensation for his losses. Again, luck was not on his side, as the court proceedings took longer than he expected. Since the matter dragged on for years, it consumed what little resources the once-successful businessman had left. The legal fees alone eroded his financial state. Although he remained determined—at least for a while—Norton eventually lost the case.

Norton's nightmare came to reality in 1858 when he had to declare bankruptcy. However, fate had another path for him. Norton would go from an influential entrepreneur to an emperor.

The Rise of Emperor Norton

After the bankruptcy, Norton was nowhere to be seen. Rumors began to circulate. Some feared for the worst while other viewed thought he might have left the city to rebuild his life elsewhere. When Norton finally reappeared in 1857, it was clear that, in addition to losing his fortune, he had lost his mental stability and sense of identity.

Norton reinvented himself in a way that was beyond anyone's imagination. He openly welcomed his eccentricity and took on the persona of Emperor Norton. He announced his rule by issuing an official proclamation. During the Gold Rush, a story about a self-proclaimed emperor would definitely draw readers and boost the newspaper's popularity. So, Norton's proclamation was published on September 17th, 1859.

The proclamation read, "At the peremptory request and desire of a large majority of the citizens of these United States, I, Joshua Norton, formerly of Algoa Bay, Cape of Good Hope, and now for the last nine years and ten months past of San Francisco, California, declare and proclaim myself Emperor of these United States."

This was only the beginning, as the American emperor would issue several more decrees throughout his reign. One the most memorable was an order for the dissolution of Congress. Dissatisfied with the political system, Norton considered Congress not only corrupt but also highly ineffective. This decree, although viewed by the higher-ups as a fantastical demand, resonated with the public who had been victims of greedy and selfish politicians.

Another one of his proclamations was the construction of a bridge between San Francisco and Oakland. The idea sounded outlandish at the time, but Norton understood the city's future needs. San Francisco was thriving and growing non-stop; the need for better connectivity was clear. Norton's vision eventually became a reality with the construction of the Bay Bridge over half a century following his death. The same thing goes for the construction of the Transbay Tube, which connects the city to Oakland by rail. Norton once decreed that the city should consider building a tunnel under San Francisco Bay, an idea that was shut down during the time but brought to life centuries later.

Norton also called for the creation of a "League of Nations." The main goal for the establishment of this league was to mediate international disputes. Just like the Bay Bridge, Norton's idea was ignored once again, only to be made into reality later on with the establishment of the League of Nations and the United Nations following World War I and WWII, respectively. Although his ideas were often framed in a whimsical manner, many agree that Emperor Norton actually had a forward-thinking approach to global issues and peacekeeping.

Norton's proclamations extended to local issues as well. Once, he issued edicts regarding proper behavior and civic pride. He urged his subjects to treat each other with respect and dignity. He even made a proclamation involving the usage of the word "Frisco." In this decree, the city emperor declared that anyone—no matter their status—who used the term "Frisco" to refer to the city would be fined twenty-five dollars. This was because he thought the nickname was a terrible insult to the thriving city.

Norton also intended to oversee the well-being and governance of a neighboring nation. He declared himself the "Protector of Mexico." Of course, no official authorities took his claim seriously.

These sets of proclamations attracted the media, although they often treated him with a mixture of amusement and mockery. Newspapers often published his edicts with a playful tone. Nevertheless, Norton appealed to the public. The citizens of San Francisco loved the charm he brought to the city and appreciated his harmless eccentricity.

Norton's appearance made him stand out. He could often be seen walking down the streets of San Francisco in a grand, though somewhat tattered, military uniform. His outfit included a plumed hat, a ceremonial sword at his side, and an umbrella or walking stick serving as a scepter.

He always made his rounds to ensure the city's sidewalks were in good condition. He even had his eyes on the police, making sure they did not sleep on the job. His work schedule was busy; the emperor took it upon himself to inspect the progress of street repairs and the construction of various buildings. Norton ensured that San Francisco's rules and regulations were adhered to by its people. He was generous with his smiles too. The emperor was not shy about interacting with the public. He talked to everyone with the same level of respect, whether they were a wealthy businessman or a street vendor.

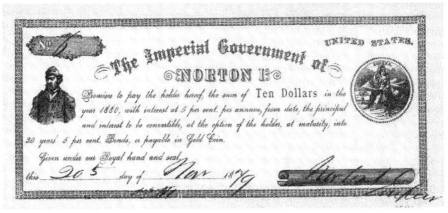

Ten dollar note issued by Norton's imperial government.[16]

Despite the teasing thrown his way by certain people, the majority of San Francisco did not mind his existence and unconventional ideas. Restaurant owners invited Norton to dine in, and transportation around the city was provided to him free of charge. At one point, the city even provided an annual sum for his needs. Norton was granted the authority to issue bonds and collect taxes from his loyal subjects. This was allowed so that he could settle any of his remaining expenses. The whimsical emperor even had his own currency, and many businesses in the city accepted these "Norton bucks" as a form of payment.

Emperor Norton in his full military regalia.[17]

Another story worth mentioning involving the emperor is a rather heartwarming one. Norton had two dogs called Lazarus and Bummer, both of which followed him while he made his rounds. These dogs were loved by the public, largely due to their aid in controlling the rat population. One day, Lazarus was caught by a dogcatcher. San Franciscans insisted upon the release of Lazarus and demanded that both dogs be allowed to roam the city freely. This reaction alone showed that Norton and his dogs had a special place in the public's eyes.

Emperor Norton "ruled" much of his kingdom through his proclamations, but he wasn't shy about addressing issues directly when needed. During one of the common anti-Chinese demonstrations of the time, Norton demonstrated his unique approach to conflict resolution. Recognizing the escalating tension at a particularly heated gathering, Norton stood before the crowd, bowed his head, and began reciting the Lord's Prayer. To the surprise of many, this act quelled the anger in the air. Perhaps feeling ashamed, the agitators dispersed without resorting to any violence.

Of course, everyone has a side that is not entirely positive. As for the emperor of San Francisco, some suggest that his stance on equal rights for women was inconsistent. In October 1878, he signed a petition to the California Constitutional Convention advocating for women's suffrage, showing his support for gender equality. However, Norton was also known to have voiced traditional views at times. During one particular women's rights lecture, Norton was given an opportunity to address the audience. Many expected him to support the cause, but instead, he did the complete opposite; he told women to stop what they were doing and return to their domestic duties.

Norton was already halfway into his life when he returned to San Francisco as an emperor. As the years passed, his health began to deteriorate. On January 8th, 1880, the self-proclaimed emperor was found dead on a street corner. He had collapsed and breathed his last before any medical help could arrive. His death was a great loss for the citizens of the city. Flags were lowered to half-mast in his honor, and many chose to close their businesses to pay their respects to Emperor Norton.

The people of San Francisco held an elaborate funeral for their beloved emperor. The wealthy residents were willing to cover the costs of both the funeral and the burial. It was said that over ten thousand people attended the funeral to pay their last respects. Norton's final resting place is in the Masonic Cemetery.

Norton's life story has been remembered and commemorated in many ways, with each shedding light on his quirky legacy. Books and biographies about the emperor exist that detail some of his out-of-the-box proclamations and his broader impacts on the busy city. The emperor is also a familiar character in the world of comics and graphic novels.

Today, San Francisco holds celebrations and tributes dedicated to Norton. People can participate in walking tours, allowing them to walk in the emperor's own footsteps to places that were significant to him. The Emperor Norton Trust is an organization that was established to preserve his legacy. Educational programs are occasionally hosted so that his story remains alive. So, while the authorities never looked at him seriously back then, his name was immortalized, and some of his ideas have been realized—perhaps his dream did come true after all.

Chapter 7 – The Forgotten Women of the Wild West

The Wild West is an extremely popular time to read about. It has often been romanticized and mythologized in literature, film, and folklore. This era, spanning from the mid-19th century to the early 20th century, conjures images of cowboys, saloons, vast ranches, revolvers, bandits, and stagecoaches.

Perhaps one thing that the media depicts correctly was the vast, untamed landscapes of the Wild West and how the West was filled with both opportunities and dangers alike. The climate of the Wild West was extreme; summers were blistering, and winters could kill. Conflicts with the Native American tribes were ever present. However, for those bold enough, the Wild West offered a chance for a new beginning. After all, this era was when rules were still being inked.

Later on, legendary figures, such as Wild Bill Hickok, Billy the Kid, and Jesse James, dominated the Wild West. Media has immortalized their stories, which are typically filled with tales of gunfights, lawlessness, and rebellion—all of which were common things that defined the American West at the time. But, of course, these men were not the only ones who dominated the West.

A cowboy of the Old West.[18]

Perhaps the phrase "It was a man's world" describes the Old West best. Even Hollywood embraces this image. Some may find Hollywood's vision of women from this era slightly confusing. Perhaps to fit in a man's world, female characters are often made to dress like men, complete with blue jeans, pointy boots, and cowboy hats. These fictional cowgirls are often armed with six-shooters hung low from their cartridge belts. This style of appearance presents the women of the Old West as strong, independent characters.

However, women of that time did not typically dress like their male counterparts. Skirts were very common among females living in the Old West. They also rode sidesaddle since riding like a man was thought to be improper. To put in simply, their appearance was rather demure and down to earth. Women also did not let their hair hang loose over their shoulders. They kept them up in neat buns. They would only let their hair down when they were at home and around their husbands or other family members.

This appearance applied to all women; even prostitutes back then donned modest Victorian clothing instead of the revealing outfits portrayed in films. It was uncommon for women to wear men's trousers, as most communities had strict laws against cross-dressing. Those who ignored this could be arrested. Perhaps this was one of the reasons why Pearl Hart was remembered by the American public back then. Most of her surviving images show her wearing men's clothing and, at times, armed with a Winchester rifle and a brace of revolvers.

Pearl Hart, the Lady Bandit of Arizona

Pearl Hart.[19]

Criminal or not, everyone has a backstory. Before she became one of the only female stagecoach robbers in the American West, Pearl Hart was born Pearl Taylor. Born in Ontario, Canada, she was brought up in a respectable middle-class family. This was quite fortunate in an era when many families struggled to make ends meet. Pearl received a good education, an opportunity not afforded to many girls at the time.

At sixteen, while studying in a boarding school, Pearl met Frederick Hart and quickly fell in love with him. It didn't take long for them to agree to elope. Frederick worked as a bartender and was also a gambler, often putting all his money on the table to satisfy his addiction. Apart from ignoring his responsibility as a provider to his wife, Frederick was also an alcoholic. To make matters worse for Pearl, her husband turned abusive.

Nevertheless, the troubled couple went on with their lives. During the Columbian Exposition, the two moved to Chicago, Illinois. Here, Frederick picked up a job, making a living as a sideshow barker. Pearl worked multiple jobs here and there.

A change began to develop when Pearl attended the Wild West shows. Here, she watched various performances that reenacted the thrill of frontier life. Pearl was especially inspired by one figure participating in the performances: Annie Oakley, who was popular for her remarkable marksmanship.

Annie Oakley.[20]

Soon, Pearl began visiting other events, including the World's Fair Women's Pavilion. Her experience there further ignited the fire in her. She spent hours listening to speeches made by a few influential women, including abolitionist and social activist Julia Ward Howe. Pearl dreamed of controlling her own destiny like these women, but the first step in doing so was to leave her abusive husband behind.

After gathering her courage, Pearl did what she had to do; she left her home and jumped on a train to Trinidad, Colorado. She built a career as a saloon singer, though this did not last for long. She later discovered that she was not alone. Pearl was pregnant with Frederick's child. This news compelled her to return to her family in Canada. However, Pearl was not planning to remain with her family. She left her son in her mother's care before setting out on a new adventure. This time around, her destination was Phoenix, Arizona.

Life was not easy in the Old West. Pearl was a cook in a café, but this was not enough to make ends meet. So, she took in laundry, hoping she could at least sustain the basic necessities. She was not the happiest, but she survived. Then, in 1895, her estranged husband reappeared. He begged her to come back and even promised to be different. He was planning on getting a regular job so that he could take better care of her. Frederick held true to his word.

After the reconciliation, the two lived a normal life, at least for a while. They explored new interests together and spent time in saloons and gambling parlors on Washington Street. This was also the period when Pearl went through another character development. Not only did she start smoking and drinking, but some also suggested that she began using drugs like marijuana and morphine.

Pearl became pregnant again, this time with a daughter. Unfortunately for Pearl, happiness was not meant to linger, as marital problems resurfaced. In 1898, a violent argument exploded between the troubled couple. He struck Pearl until she fell unconscious. Frederick left his wife again and joined Roosevelt's Rough Riders in Cuba. Pearl, who was still pregnant, returned to her family. History repeated itself again; she left her daughter with her family and set off to Arizona.

It is safe to say that this was her lowest point. While she did find work in various mining camps, it was challenging for a lone woman to survive in the Wild West. She became so depressed that she attempted to take her own life more than once.

Life was better for Pearl in 1899. Fate led her to a miner named Joe Boot, whose charm captivated her. However, life had another piece of misfortune for Pearl. Not long after her meeting with Boot, Pearl received news from her brother. Their mother had fallen gravely ill, and the family was suffering from mounting medical bills. Desperate, Pearl turned to Boot for advice, who offered a few interesting ideas about how to earn some quick cash. Pearl had to abandon her moral compass and start embracing a life of crime.

Perhaps seeing no other way, Pearl agreed, and the two started planning. Their first scheme was simple but daring. First, Pearl seduced and lured a couple of men into their room by promising them a few hours of romance. Blinded by desire, the unsuspecting men did not object and let their guard down. Little did they know, Boot was hiding in the shadows, waiting for the right moment to knock the men out cold. Once unconscious, Pearl and Boot quickly searched them for money and valuables. Although this scheme rewarded them with some cash, it was far from enough. The pair needed to plan something bigger and bolder—a stagecoach robbery.

They chose a stagecoach that took the route between Florence and Globe, Arizona. For this ambitious heist, Pearl decided to disguise herself. She cut off her hair and wore one of Boot's outfits. The plan was set into motion on May 30th, 1899.

They leaped from their hiding spot into the middle of the path when the stagecoach approached. The driver was taken by surprise, especially since the pair had their guns drawn. While Boot kept his aim on the driver, Pearl went around and ordered the passengers out of the coach. She shouted for them to empty their pockets and wallets. Pearl collected the valuables—cash amounting to $450 (worth approximately $15,000 today) and a revolver. After ordering the terrified passengers back into the coach, Boot fired his gun into the air. With haste, the driver took off while the pair galloped into the wilderness.

However, the two were unfamiliar with the unforgiving desert terrain. They wandered for days, hopelessly lost. The two finally made camp under a grove of trees. In the morning, they found they were no longer alone. Boot and Pearl found themselves surrounded by the authorities.

They were brought to jail in Globe. Much to her surprise, Pearl had unknowingly made a name for herself. Crowds gathered around to take even the shortest glimpse at the infamous "Bandit Queen." They wanted to see the woman who was bold enough to defy societal norms and experience the adventures that the frontier promised.

Pearl embraced her newfound fame. She was said to have always entertained her admirers, even giving away autographs. She was also more than happy to share her tales with those who asked.

This was not the end of her journey. She and another prisoner named Ed Hogan attempted to escape from jail. Her reputation grew tremendously, though freedom was beyond her reach. Pearl was eventually recaptured and locked up in her cell yet again.

Pearl's trial was held in Florence in November 1899. It was a spectacle. She boldly insisted the court had no right to try her since her gender never once gave her a voice in the laws governing her fate. She admitted her guilt but told the story of her tragically ill mother, whom she was trying to help. Her lawyer also argued that Pearl had been a law-abiding citizen until she became desperate to help her mother. The jury was sympathetic, but the magistrate was not. Believing Pearl had manipulated the jury with her charms, he ordered a retrial and charged her with unlawfully carrying a gun. Without the jury's sympathy, Pearl Hart was eventually convicted and sentenced to five years in the Yuma Territorial Prison.

As for Joe Boot, he was also sentenced to prison. He managed to stage a successful escape in 1901. His name doesn't appear again in the history books after that.

Pearl was more of a celebrity in prison than a criminal. Reporters often visited her, asking her to narrate her adventures. Pearl embraced the attention and loved posing for photographs. On December 19th, 1902, she was paroled. She hoped to capitalize on her celebrity status when she moved to Kansas City, but unfortunately, public interest in the "Lady Bandit" had waned.

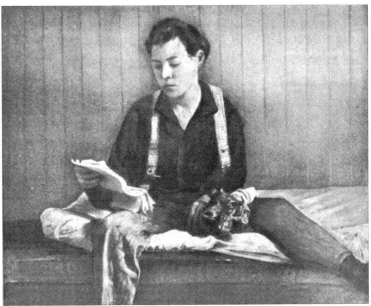

Pearl Hart in her cell.[31]

Pearl went incognito afterward. Her name was no longer in the newspapers until she was arrested in Kansas City. This time around, she was using the alias Mrs. L. P. Keele, and she was taken into custody for purchasing stolen goods. Later, she vanished again, resurfacing briefly in 1924 in the old courthouse in Florence.

What happened in her later life remains unknown. While some said she operated a cigar store in Kansas City and eventually passed away in 1925, others claim she moved to San Francisco and died much later, in 1952. Another popular theory explains how Pearl found her soulmate in Dripping Springs, Arizona. Here, Pearl and her husband lived the rest of their days as ranchers. She went by the name Pearl Bywater and was said to have passed away in 1956.

Madame Mustache, the Renowned Gambler Across the West

In the lawless American frontier, gambling held a prominent place in society. The Old West was a land of opportunity and danger. Fortunes were made and lost on the turn of a card or the roll of a die. Games like poker, faro, roulette, and vingt-et-un (the precursor to blackjack) became very popular. Saloons and gambling parlors sprang up in every burgeoning town, becoming social hubs. The lure of easy money and the thrill of risk-taking drew men from all walks of life to these establishments. They also sought to escape the harsh realities of frontier life, if only for a night.

Skilled gamblers were both feared and revered, their reputations spreading far and wide. Amid this backdrop of high stakes and high tension, one figure stood out, not just for her gambling prowess but also for her charm and unconventional path. Her name was Eleanore Dumont, but she is better known as Madame Mustache.

Eleanore Dumont's journey from France to America began with dreams of adventure and prosperity. Born as Simone Jules, she left behind her old life, adopted a new name, and ventured into the unpredictable world of the Wild West. Eleanore quickly established herself as a gambler, favoring the

Eleanore Dumont, c. 1860s.[22]

game of vingt-et-un, which showcased her sharp intellect.

Eleanore's first gambling parlor was in Nevada City. Specific details about her funding vary, but it is widely believed that Eleanore gained the necessary capital through a combination of savings from prior ventures, investments, and loans from influential and wealthy figures in the mining town who were impressed by her vision and charisma.

Her establishment was a sight to behold. It was rather sophisticated, especially since it was located in a rough-and-tumble mining town. She made sure to furnish it with the most expensive carpets and elegant gas chandeliers. Unlike the other gambling dens in the town, Eleanore's parlor had a strict rule of welcoming only groomed and well-behaved men. Even cursing was heavily discouraged.

It did not take long for Eleanore to see a profit. She successfully amassed enough capital to expand her business. After partnering with a professional New York gambler named David Tobin, Eleanore launched another parlor. Named Dumon's Palace, it was yet another success. However, Eleanore had to relocate to another location once the gold in the town ran out. In 1857, she found herself in Columbia, California. Here, she set up her table in a local hotel.

A few years later, Eleanore decided to leave the gambling business behind. Though she knew little about ranching, she bought a ranch in Carson City, Nevada, hoping for a quieter life. However, her life changed when she met Jack McKnight. McKnight was said to be a handsome man and a sweet talker. Eleanore quickly fell for him. However, McKnight was far from a chivalrous gentleman—or rather, a *knight* in shining armor. He was a con man. In just the span of a short month, he managed to get his hands on Eleanore's money. He sold her ranch, leaving her with only debts and despair. According to legend, Eleanore successfully tracked the con man down. She took revenge by killing him with a double blast from a shotgun.

Due to her devastating financial state, Eleanore was left with no choice but to return to the mining camps, where she took up gambling again. She found herself in Pioche, Nevada, in 1861 and moved from one gold camp to another for the next twenty years.

Time took its toll on Eleanore's appearance. A dark line of hair appeared on her upper lip. She gained the nickname "Madame Mustache." Her eyes, which once glistened with hope and life, gradually dimmed as the years passed. Plus, the environment in the mining camps was rough. Spending decade after decade in these towns affected her.

Men cursed freely in her presence and told dirty jokes in front of her. Eleanore grew accustomed to the atmosphere, and she even started to use coarse language in her daily conversations.

During these difficult times, Eleanore ventured into another business. She started operating brothels. She realized that the men who visited her gambling establishments often looked for more than just a game. This new venture contributed to her already growing influence and financial success. Her brothels were kept clean and well maintained.

Eleanore soon began a target of several outlaws due to her reputation. Once, two robbers confronted her as she was leaving one of her establishments. They demanded her purse, but Eleanore remained calm. Looking straight into the men's eyes, she firmly told them that they would not take her belongings. The robbers were taken aback by her bravery; after all, not many women would dare to speak back to them, especially when they were alone.

Eleanore reached into her handbag, leading the robbers to think that she was reaching for money. Instead, she pulled out a small derringer and fired point-blank at one of the men. He dropped to the ground, writhing in pain. The other robber turned on his heels and ran. Once again, Eleanore had proved that she was not a woman to be played with.

Apart from her tales of bravery, Eleanore retained her good heart. Beneath her tough exterior, she was still fond of kindness and generosity. Madame Mustache could often be seen providing meals and even a place to stay for troubled, hardworking miners.

Eleanore's final stop was Bodie, California. Here, she was said to have borrowed $300 from a friend to open a table. However, in just a few hours, misfortune struck; she lost everything. Her story came to an end on September 8th, 1879, when her body was found lying just outside of town. At her side was a note that expressed her weariness of life. She had taken her own life.

The Life of Josephine Earp

Josephine Earp in her youth.[23]

Josephine Sarah Marcus (simply known as "Josie") led a life that was rather different compared to those of Pearl Hart and Eleanore Dumont. Her story was more about the adaptability that defined many women of the Old West. Josephine was born in New York City to Jewish parents. Little is known about her childhood.

She began longing for a change in 1879 when the Pauline Markham Theater Company came to town. She witnessed the glamor and adventure surrounding the traveling troupe. It did not take long for Josephine to begin dreaming of living a life full of excitement every single day. One day, she made the decision to leave the comfort of her home. She slipped away with the troupe and left her family without uttering a goodbye. She took one more glance at the familiar streets of New York before leaving for good. Her destination was Arizona.

In Arizona, Josephine met a charming yet troubled man. His name was Johnny Behan, and he was popularly known in the town for his silver tongue and dashing appearance. Although he was divorced and a bankrupt politician, Josephine found the man captivating. They formed a romantic relationship that was fraught with both passion and drama.

Josephine's family grew worried about her well-being. They tried tracking her down and successfully brought her back to New York.

However, Josephine did not remain in New York for long. By May 1880, she was already back in Arizona. She had made the decision to join her lover, Johnny, in Tombstone, a busy silver mining town. Despite their romance, the two never married.

Much to Josephine's disappointment, Johnny Behan was a man of gambling, drinking, and infidelity. Their relationship was strained, and it did not help that Johnny kept giving Josephine empty promises.

Josephine eventually crossed paths with another man, one who would remain by her side to her final days. Known as Wyatt Earp, he was a popular lawman with a storied past. In Josephine's eyes, Wyatt was the complete opposite of Johnny. Apart from being committed to justice, Wyatt was steady and resolute. The two soon became attracted to each other.

Although Josephine was still with Johnny, she met Wyatt several times to the point where a stronger bond was formed between them. Some said it was Josephine's spirit that attracted the lawman the most. Nevertheless, Josephine gave Johnny a chance to mend their issues, yet Johnny had no plans on changing himself. So, Josephine put an end to their relationship in early to mid-1811.

Wyatt Earp and Jonny Behan were no strangers. Their relationship was not friendly, though. They were rivals. After all, both were well-known figures in Tombstone. Most of the time, their conflicts were so big that they affected their personal lives. Their rivalry reached a climax with the infamous gunfight at the O.K. Corral on October 26th, 1881. The confrontation was violent. It was between the Earp brothers (including their loyal ally Doc Holliday) and the Clanton-McLaury gang (which included Johnny Behan's associates). Although the gunfight lasted only thirty seconds, the aftermath was terrible; three of the Clanton-McLaury gang members died. Wyatt survived, and his legendary status grew even bigger.

The relationship between Josephine and Wyatt also grew following the gunfight. However, this is not a fairytale. The Earp brothers were struck with another tragedy five months later. On March 18th, 1882, their brother, Morgan Earp, was shot in the back as he played pool at a saloon. This ambush undeniably shocked the siblings. Morgan's body was transported by the brothers back to their parent's house in Colton,

California. The Earps believed this injustice deserved nothing but revenge. The Earp brothers, along with Doc Holliday, went down the road of vengeance, which later became known as the Earp Vendetta Ride. They pursued and killed those who they suspected to be responsible for the ambush, including Ike Clanton (who was present during the O.K. Corral Gunfight but did not participate in it).

Although the road to revenge was a rough one, Josephine stood by Wyatt's side. She was his source of support and solace. Their relationship flourished and would endure for nearly fifty years.

With the Vendetta Ride over, Josephine and Wyatt went on a series of adventures across the Old West. Their early ventures included running saloons in San Diego, California. They also tried their luck in real estate during the late 1880s. Opportunities would dry up, and another window opened. The two moved from one location to another promising one. They were the epitome of the restless energy of the American frontier.

The pair also moved to Nome, Alaska, during the Klondike Gold Rush in the early 1900s. Again, they invested in saloons and gambling establishments, hoping to make a fortune.

In the early 1920s, they moved to Los Angeles, a bustling and rapidly growing city. Wyatt Earp got into the real estate business, but he also attempted to get into the film industry. He tried to produce silent films about the Wild West, though his efforts were not very successful.

Josephine and her husband Wyatt in their later years.[24]

Josephine Marcus remained loyal to Wyatt Earp until the end of his life. Wyatt eventually passed away on January 13th, 1929. Josephine worked hard to preserve his legacy. Her goal was to ensure that his story was told to the future generations accurately. Josephine did not mind battling with a group of writers or filmmakers who wished to change Wyatt's adventures or even his characters and personality.

Josephine finally passed away on December 19th, 1944. She lived a life of adventure until the age of eighty-three. Her remains were buried in the Hills of Eternity Cemetery (located in Colma, California) alongside Wyatt Earp. Even after death, the pair was inseparable.

Chapter 8 – The Great Boston Molasses Flood: A Sticky Disaster

The date was January 15th, 1919. It was just another normal day in Boston's North End. The sun was up, its golden rays shining over the narrow streets. However, the air still had its winter chill. A group of children who had just been released from Michelangelo School made their way down the street. One of them was Anthony di Stasio, who was walking hand in hand with his four other sisters. The children's laughter filled the air, as did the sound of horses' hooves on the cobblestone streets.

Suddenly, a faint rumble could be heard. No one minded the noise at first, but as it grew slightly louder, people started to look around. Even Anthony stopped to try to locate the source of the peculiar noise. The children's laughter was now gone, replaced by a loud rumble and screams. In the distance, a wall of dark, glistening liquid came crashing through the streets, almost similar to a tsunami.

"Run!" Anthony screamed to his sisters, but it was too late. The thick wave of molasses was faster than they expected. It hit them with the force of a tidal wave. The children were immediately swept off their feet. Anthony struggled to keep his head above the molasses. The sweet scent of the thick liquid filled his nostrils, and the heaviness of the syrup pulled him down.

The wave devoured everything in its path, from children to adults. The molasses even engulfed twenty horses that had been peacefully munching hay in their stalls. They whined and tried to get out of the sticky torrent, yet they were helpless. In the end, only one horse survived. However, its wounds were so severe that the vet had no choice but to euthanize it.

Buildings were not spared from this unrelenting, sticky flood. Windows were shattered, and wood splintered when the molasses slammed into them. Boston's North End had completely changed. Debris could be seen floating on the sticky brown sea, dead bodies underneath the liquid, and buildings either completely in ruins of half destroyed.

Anthony could hear his mother calling his name, yet it was faint. He had no idea where he was. He tried screaming for help, but the molasses clogged his throat the moment he opened his mouth.

Then, the wave finally subsided. Anthony was now on the ground. There were creaking sounds of partly destroyed buildings, some of which were seconds away from collapsing. He could hear the faint weeps of the people around him. Finally, Anthony was able to open his eyes. His vision blurred when three familiar faces hovered above him. Although there was relief on their faces, horror was also visible.

"Thank God," one of his sisters whispered as tears rolled down her cheeks.

Anthony blinked multiple times to clear his vision. However, he could only see three of his sisters.

The flood was a disaster of historic magnitude. Witnesses said that the towering wave reached heights of up to twenty-five feet when it came through the streets of Boston. This dark syrup was able to submerge parts of the city two to three feet deep. The molasses traveled down the streets with an unimaginable speed of thirty-five miles per hour.

Of course, every tragedy has a cause. As for this particular catastrophe, it all began with the Purity Distilling Company facility at 529 Commercial Street near Keany Square. The company was a subsidiary of United States Industrial Alcohol (USIA). It had been storing vast quantities of molasses in its massive steel tank, which was intended for the production of industrial alcohol. To contain such a large amount of molasses, the tank had to be a colossal structure. It stood fifty feet tall and ninety feet in diameter. It was able to contain about 2.3 million gallons of molasses.

A number of factors contributed to the tank's disastrous failure. First, there was an issue with the temperature. The temperature had increased sharply from the extreme cold of the preceding days to an unusually warm forty degrees Fahrenheit. This abrupt change in temperature caused the molasses, which had previously been thick and sluggish in the cold, to become more liquid-like. The creation of carbon dioxide during fermentation within the tank made things worse, as it raised the internal pressure. The increased fluidity, combined with the high pressure in the tank, was too much for the structure to handle.

The molasses tank before the explosion.[25]

Researchers also blame the poor construction of the tank. The tank's walls were built too thin, so it failed to withstand the immense weight and pressure of the thick liquid. To make matters worse, the rivets in the tank's construction were found to be poorly secured. Arthur Jell was the man responsible for overseeing the construction of the tank. There were already several signs of a catastrophe about to happen, yet he chose to neglect basic safety tests. He even ignored the danger signs coming from the tank every time it was filled.

Prohibition played a role in the events that led to the tragedy. Prohibition was a nationwide restriction on alcohol in the United States, established by the Eighteenth Amendment to the Constitution. This amendment was enacted on January 16th, 1919, and made it unlawful to produce, sell, or transport alcoholic beverages beginning in 1920. Thus, investigators suspected that the Purity Distilling Company wanted to convert as much molasses into alcohol as possible before the ban took effect. The company increased the frequency and volume of molasses shipments to the tank, pushing it to its limits.

As for Anthony di Stasio, he learned that his sister, Maria, was among those who had perished in the tragedy. The news hit him like a second wave, and it was probably more devastating than the first. However, Maria was not the only victim. Twenty more bodies were later discovered, including another ten-year-old child.

As soon as the situation was under control, rescue operations began. Under the command of Lieutenant Commander H. J. Copeland, 116 cadets from the Massachusetts Nautical School (now called the Massachusetts Maritime Academy) sprang into action. From the nearby pier (they were initially aboard the USS *Nantucket*), these brave cadets sprinted as fast as they could toward the location of the tragedy. Curious bystanders also flocked to the scene, but the cadets kept them at bay. This was done so that the public would not interfere in the mission, as that could possibly lead to another accident.

The aftermath of the Boston Molasses disaster.[26]

More assistance arrived later on, including the Red Cross, the Army, and the Boston Police Department. The nurses worked through the night; about 150 survivors had to be treated. Due to the large number of casualties, makeshift hospitals had to be prepared in nearby buildings.

The rescue mission was challenging largely because of the thick and sticky properties of the molasses. Rescuers found it hard to move, and freeing victims from the syrup required substantial effort. The search for victims took four days.

Identifying the deceased was another challenge. The bodies were glazed almost completely with the thick, brown syrup. Even their family members needed some time to recognize them.

The molasses seeped into everything, including subway platforms and streets. It was unimaginably sticky in hundreds of homes, payphones, and train cars. The environmental and economic impact on the neighborhood and the city itself was immense. It took months to clear the thick, sticky sludge that covered the streets and buildings of Boston's busy North End. Plant life was also impacted by the molasses. It had contaminated the soil as it seeped into the ground. Numerous laborers and substantial resources were needed for the cleanup, diverting money and time away from other important local projects.

Local businesses were among those that had to pay for the tragedy. Business owners found both their goods and shops completely ruined. They were left with no other choice but to halt their operations. This catastrophe disrupted the transportation system around the city as well, as train lines and subway platforms had be cleaned thoroughly before they could operate. While some businesses were able to bounce back, many others never fully recovered.

The damaged elevated railway caused by the disaster.[27]

The disaster was not the cause of Mother Nature. Thus, victims and their families were intent on taking the matter to court. They filed a class-action lawsuit against USIA, accusing them of negligence in the construction and maintenance of the molasses tank. The trial went on for over five years. Evidence poured in showing how the tank had not been thoroughly examined and improperly built. According to a testimony, it was revealed that Arthur Jell had no background in engineering or architecture. He was also confirmed to have disregarded multiple signs of the tank's instability.

Another shocking piece of evidence revealed that the tank had already leaked from the start—a direct indication that it was not structurally sound. Nevertheless, the USIA ignored this and continued to use the tank. Reports of workers being advised to overlook leaks and odd noises coming from the tank—which was painted brown to conceal the continuous molasses drips—further exposed the company's incompetence.

The court ruled in favor of the plaintiffs; USIA was responsible for the accident. As a result, the company was ordered to compensate the victims and their families for what they had to go through. This ruling was a major win for the survivors. It also established a precedent for holding businesses accountable for their misconduct. Because of this disaster, industrial safety standards were improved.

The story of this heartbreaking tragedy continues to be passed down through the generations, though many outside of Boston are not very familiar with it. Memorials and historical markers have been built as a tribute to the victims. Although the catastrophe happened many years ago, some claim that the subtle scent of molasses still lingers in the air, especially when summer arrives.

Chapter 9 – The Battle of the Little Bighorn and Beyond

Many may agree that the westward expansion of the United States, which took place in the 19th century, was one of the most important chapters in American history. This expansion was driven by a number of factors, but it was mainly due to economic opportunities. At the time, every nation across the globe was in a race that had no finishing line; everyone wanted to bring their economies to new heights. Thus, it was not a surprise when the American settlers chose to turn their gaze westward, where there were fertile lands for various crops to thrive and a treasure trove of gold and other precious minerals.

These American settlers held the idea of Manifest Destiny close to their hearts. They believed that they were destined by God to spread their civilization across the continent. The Homestead Act of 1862 led settlers to flock to the unfamiliar lands of the West; the act provided them free land as long as they were willing to cultivate it.

The settlers were given a chance at a new beginning and the potential to create a fortune should they move west. However, the expansion really only benefited one side. The Native American tribes, which had long called these lands their home, had to pay the price.

November 27th, 1868, is a date to remember. It was the day when General George Armstrong Custer led his 7th Cavalry toward a small village along the Washita River. The inhabitants were the Southern Cheyenne tribe.

When the first rays of sunlight shone through the skies, Custer ordered his men to charge. The cavalry did not hold back. They overwhelmed the village and decimated not only the warriors of the Southern Cheyenne but also innocent women and children. Those who survived faced capture. The entire village was burned. Custer also ordered his men to destroy the tribe's winter supplies.

The Battle of the Washita made it into the history books; it is often known as the first substantial victory for the Americans in the American Indian Wars. To the settlers, the aftermath of the battle was a triumph of civilization over savagery. They were one step closer to achieving their destiny. However, to the Cheyenne, it was a bloody massacre.

The settlers offered treaties to the Native American tribes. However, these were nothing more than just signatures and words inked on paper. The treaties were broken repeatedly, and encroachment on tribal lands resumed. Tensions were ever present in the West, and conflicts were inevitable.

Another important date was June 25th, 1876. The key player on the American side of the battlefield was once again General Custer. This time around, the battle took place amidst the rolling hills of Montana near the Little Bighorn River. Based on his previous successes, Custer was confident. He was ignorant to the fact that this very battle would become known as Custer's Last Stand.

The famous general and his forces met their fate near this river. Despite losing the battle, this moment earned a spot in American history. For years, Custer and his forces were hailed as heroes. They died heroically in an attempt to end the so-called savagery in the untamed West. Many textbooks portrayed him as an American legend.

However, it is almost impossible to separate bias from history. Records were often written by the victors. They wrote in a manner to obscure the truth. Custer's wife spent her life ensuring that her husband's name would not be forgotten. For many decades, the narrative of the Battle of the Little Bighorn centered on the general, while the Native American perspectives of the battle were often neglected.

The Battle of the Little Bighorn in the Eyes of the Natives

According to the accounts of the Native Americans, the story begins with a gathering of leaders from the Lakota, Northern Cheyenne, and Arapaho tribes. A figure rose before the rest. This man was Sitting Bull, a highly respected holy man of the Hunkpapa Lakota. With a firm voice, he encouraged his people to fight.

"Think not for yourselves but our ancestors and children!" he said. "This land is our beating heart. We have to defend it with our lives."

His people roared in agreement, including Crazy Horse, a revered Oglala Lakota war leader. There was a sense of strong unity among the tribes; they were determined to face the settlers and protect what was theirs. They began preparing for the imminent war.

A few weeks was all they had. Sitting Bull performed the Sun Dance for two days with no rest, hoping the ancestors would grant him a vision that could guide his people to victory. The ritual, however, was not for the weak. It was believed that Sitting Bull also sacrificed a hundred pieces of flesh cut from his arm for the ceremony.

As the sun scorched the earth on the final day of the ceremony, Sitting Bull began to stumble and eventually collapsed. He might have appeared unconscious to the people around him, but Sitting Bull was allegedly witnessing a vision.

When he regained consciousness, Sitting Bull rushed to inform his people of what he had seen. In his vision, he saw dozens of soldiers pouring into a village. The state of these soldiers caught his attention. They charged into the village in an upside-down position, which was interpreted as a good omen. It was a clear sign that victory was theirs.

The day finally came. On June 25th, 1876, the Native Americans could hear the distant thunder of hooves as the invaders made their move toward the Little Bighorn. While Custer and his 7th Cavalry were bolstered by their previous victories, the Native Americans were inspired by Sitting Bull's vision. Knowing that the spirit of their ancestors was with them, their morale and resolve were extremely high.

The American cavalry approached head-on, only to be met with a strong wall of resistance. The brave warriors, led by Crazy Horse, moved swiftly to combat the invaders. Battle cries pierced the air as the Native Americans charged valiantly against the enemy that had been encroaching on their lands.

The Native Americans executed a strategic set of flanking maneuvers and surrounded the American cavalrymen. The warriors cut off their retreat and outnumbered them. It is safe to say that Custer's cavalry was caught off guard, and panic began to consume them. They struggled to maintain their lines as the Native American warriors continuously charged.

The Native American warriors decimating Custer's cavalry.[28]

The 7th Cavalry could not achieve victory unless there was some kind of divine intervention. They were decimated by the end of the day; even Custer himself lay lifeless on the bloodied battlefield.

This victory might appear to be just another military triumph, but it was far more than that in the eyes of the Native Americans. Their success was a symbol of resistance and a strong piece of evidence that their spirit could not easily be broken.

A Cheyenne artist's depiction of the Battle of the Little Bighorn.[29]

However, the Battle of the Little Bighorn left behind a tragic consequence for the tribes. While they rejoiced in their success, the US government made a move to intensify its military campaigns. Convinced by the need to crush the Native American resistance once and for all, the government launched a relentless pursuit of the Native Americans, especially their leaders. More troops poured into the western lands, and the government invested more resources in the mission. Over the next few months, more forced relocations occurred, and skirmishes became incredibly common.

Undeterred, Sitting Bull and Crazy Horse continued their resistance, although the military might of the US government proved to be too overwhelming for them. Crazy Horse was captured in 1877 and brought to Camp Robinson in Nebraska. The Battle of the Little Bighorn had happened not even a year prior. Crazy Horse was eventually killed by a bayonet in September 1877 as he attempted to avoid imprisonment.

Sitting Bull, on the other hand, succeeded in avoiding capture for several years. He even managed to lead a number of his people to Canada. Here, the survivors were given a chance to seek refuge and, hopefully, find peace. Unfortunately, life was not easy for them in Canada. The government could not provide them with long-term support since its resources were limited. So, Sitting Bull was left with no choice but to return to the United States in 1881. He finally surrendered after the relentless pursuit by the authorities. He hoped that by handing himself in that his people would be spared and given food.

Sitting Bull was made a prisoner of war for two years. He was released in 1883 to join the rest of his people at the Standing Rock Reservation in present-day South Dakota, where he lived under the watchful eyes of Indian agents. Sitting Bull was no longer a military threat in the eyes of the US government, but his immense influence worried the authorities.

Tensions rose again in 1890 when the US government received news of the Ghost Dance movement. Officials were afraid that another uprising would take place. Although Sitting Bull did not actively participate in the Ghost Dance movement, the authorities were still suspicious of him. On December 15th, 1890, the government handed out orders to the Indian agents. They were to surround Sitting Bull's cabin. This was the end of the road for Sitting Bull, as he was shot and killed following a struggle.

The Apache and Geronimo

This was not the only time that the Native Americans fiercely showed their defiance. It happened often, but let's take a look far to the south where the Apache lived. Here, the authorities had to keep an eye on a certain man named Geronimo.

Like many other Native American tribes, the Apache had been embroiled in several skirmishes with the US government. These are known as the Apache Wars. It all began in the early 1850s, back when the United States were trying to expand its territory after the Mexican-American War. As a result of the Treaty of Guadalupe Hidalgo in 1848, large portions of what is now the American Southwest were ceded to the US. These regions included lands traditionally inhabited by the Apache.

The Apache experienced pressure from Mexican and American settlers. These pressures escalated into skirmishes when gold was discovered in California and other parts of the West. The violence and encroachments never left the Apache too discouraged. The Apache were skilled warriors, and all of them possessed an exceptional knowledge of the harsh desert terrain. They often employed guerrilla tactics against their enemies before disappearing into the untamed wilderness. However, the more success these Native Americans achieved, the harsher the measures taken by the US military. They knew they had to subdue any Apache who defied them, so they chose to resort to merciless tactics, including scorched earth tactics.

It was during this period of hardship that Geronimo managed to carve his name as a legendary figure. Born in what is now Arizona in 1829, Geronimo spent his early life surrounded by the rugged beauty of the desert. Geronimo's rise to defiance began in 1858 when Mexican soldiers poured into his camp. They murdered his wife, children, and mother. This loss undoubtedly ignited a fire of vengeance and hatred within him. His hatred, however, was not without a course; he only wished to display his defiance to those who sought to destroy more of his people. And so, he vowed to keep fighting and chasing the invaders out of his ancestors' lands until his very last breath.

Geronimo (on the right) in 1886, alongside three other Apache warriors.[30]

Geronimo led his people in many bold raids. His knowledge of the terrain combined with his strategic thinking were a gift, and he was able to evade capture multiple times. While the Native American warriors revered him, he was soon branded as one of the biggest threats by the US military.

He further eroded his relationship with the US government in the mid-1880s. The Apache leader was not content at being confined to a reservation. He daringly escaped the reservation he had been forced on, bringing along a few of his most loyal followers. The group embarked on another mission of resistance. They made use of their ability to hit and run, keeping the US Army on its toes. Geronimo successfully evaded capture for years.

However, it is nearly impossible for a person to live a life on the lam. Exhaustion and dwindling supplies led to Geronimo and his warriors handing themselves in to General Nelson A. Miles in September 1886. They were then transported to Fort Bowie, Arizona, before moving to Fort Pickens in Pensacola, Florida. The harsh conditions of the forts they were held in took a toll on their health.

In 1887, Geronimo and his warriors faced another relocation. The US military wished to put them as far away from their homeland as possible. They were taken to Mount Vernon Barracks in Alabama and later, in 1894, to Fort Sill in present-day Oklahoma. Here, Geronimo and his warriors spent the remainder of their lives.

Although Geromino remained a prisoner of war until the end of his life, his influence was widely known. Apart from having his own autobiography (*Geronimo's Story of His Life*), he was also allowed to appear at various public events, such as the 1904 St. Louis World's Fair and President Theodore Roosevelt's inauguration in 1905. He eventually converted to Christianity in 1903, although he was also said to have had mixed feelings about the religion.

Geronimo died on February 17th, 1909, possibly due to pneumonia.

Geronimo's grave at Fort Sill.[31]

Many would agree that these Native American uprisings left a huge impact on society. Although these acts of resistance were eventually quelled, they showed the dissatisfaction and struggles of the Native Americans. Their populations were significantly reduced, and many survivors were forced to relocate. Treaties were constantly broken, and the settlers disrupted their traditional ways of life.

These stories of resistance reflect the pride and unity of Native American communities. To this day, legal battles for land rights are ongoing. Numerous efforts are being undertaken to address historical grievances and lost lands.

Chapter 10 – The Black Wall Street Massacre

Three decades after the abolition of slavery, African Americans were still very familiar with injustice. The promises of freedom and equality proved to be nothing more than empty words in many parts of the country with the introduction of Jim Crow laws. These laws were put into place following the Reconstruction era. They were intended to impose racial segregation and maintain White supremacy. Many Whites were in favor of the Jim Crow laws as they saw it as a necessary measure to maintain social order and prevent racial mixing.

Those of color were placed at the lowest level of the hierarchy. African Americans were treated as second-class citizens. Because of the Jim Crow laws, they had to live a life controlled by social and legal limitations. It was common to find signs that read "Whites Only" or "Colored." Racial segregation applied to public parks, schools, public transportation, and even restrooms.

Although the world had advanced, racism and prejudice remained. African Americans were not only denied basic rights, but many were also denied opportunities to achieve a better life.

Sign for the "colored" waiting room at a bus station in Durham, North Carolina, c. 1940.[32]

The Beginning of Greenwood

O. W. Gurley was the son of two liberated slaves. From a young age, Gurley had a vision. He wanted to overcome the limitations that was imposed by his race. Perhaps thanks to his parents who taught him the value of education and hard work, Gurley taught himself how to read and write.

As he stepped into the world as a young adult, Gurley became a teacher. His love for education made him eager to share its value with the younger generation. Education, however, was not his only passion. He had ambition and a great entrepreneurial spirit. So, he decided to seek out greater opportunities. Gurley eventually earned a spot working with the US Postal Service, which was a stable and well-paying position for a Black man at the time.

Nevertheless, his heart was not content. At the age of twenty-five, Gurley participated in the Cherokee Outlet Opening. This land run saw thousands of settlers racing to claim plots of land in what is now Oklahoma. The event was not for the faint of heart. Settlers used every means possible to stake their claims. Some rode horses and drove carts, and some ran on foot. As for Gurley and his wife, Emma, they had to run fifty miles before finally arriving at an area of prairie grass. Here, they staked a claim, which would soon become known as Perry, Oklahoma.

After his successful land claim, Gurley went on to run for the position of county treasurer. This did not work out, though he never stopped contributing to his community. He took up the mantle as the principal of the town's school and operated a general store for at least a decade.

In 1905, Gurley made a bold move. He heard news of huge oil fields in the nearby boomtown of Tulsa. Recognizing the importance of oil, Gurley knew there was a potential for him to contribute more. He purchased a piece of land on the north side of the Frisco train tracks, where Gurley began his grand plan. He came up with the blueprints of a city where African Americans could thrive.

Knowing that Tulsa would soon receive a wave of freed slaves and sharecroppers, Gurley opened a grocery store to provide them with essentials. This was the beginning of Greenwood Avenue. Gurley then split his land into a number of lots, which were then turned into homes and businesses. These lots were sold exclusively to African Americans. His vision was gradually turning into reality. The district showed convincing signs of growth.

As expected, Tulsa boomed in the first two decades of the 20th century. It transformed from a dusty little town into a flourishing metropolis. Tulsa was named the world's oil capital, and its population skyrocketed.

Greenwood also underwent an impressive transformation. By 1920, the district had expanded to include over thirty-five city blocks. Greenwood was a melting pot of entrepreneurs. It even earned the nickname "Black Wall Street." John Williams and his wife Loula were some of the many successful entrepreneurs who thrived in Greenwood. They owned a confectionery store, and the two later built the Dreamland Theater. Another familiar name in the community was Simon Berry. He was the mastermind behind the transportation network (which included Ford Model Ts and buses) from Greenwood to downtown Tulsa. Once his business grew, Berry expanded his services to include chartering jets for Tulsa's wealthy oilmen.

The district even had its own publications, such as the *Tulsa Star*, which was the brainchild of A. J. Smitherman. This form of media, along with other local publications, helped Greenwood residents stay informed and connected.

Greenwood had turned into a proper city. It boasted nearly everything. There were pool halls, auto repair shops, beauty salons, a roller-skating rink, several grocery stores, barber shops, and also funeral homes. Its residents were also free to make use of community amenities, including a hospital and a US Post Office substation.

Economically, Greenwood was doing exceptionally well. Businesses supported each other, so every dollar spent in the district was circulated within the community nearly thirty times. Greenwood also had residents who held religion close to their hearts. Several churches found a home in the district, with the most famous one being the Mt. Zion Baptist Church.

Education was prioritized in the community. An elite high school was even built in Greenwood. Named after Booker T. Washington (one of the most influential African American educators), the school featured an extensive curriculum aimed to prepare its students to enter esteemed universities. They were taught a range of subjects ranging from English, science, and art to ancient history, Latin, and algebra. Some of the highest-paid professionals in Greenwood were teachers.

As for O. W. Gurley, his journey did not end with the establishment of Greenwood. As the district gained more influence, he took the chance to expand his ventures. Some of his earnings came from renting out a few buildings of his own—three brick apartment buildings and five townhouses located close to his grocery store. Another portion of his fortune came from the Gurley Hotel and the Masonic Lodge. He also had a business in the employment agency, which focused on migrant workers. Gurley was assigned as the sheriff's deputy, giving him the power to police the Black community. At his height, Gurley was worth more than $150,000, which would roughly be $5 million in today's currency.

Greenwood was home to another influential figure. J. B. Stradford was a prominent lawyer and businessman. He owned the Stradford Hotel, a famous stop among Black travelers. The hotel was so luxurious that it earned a reputation nationwide. It was popularly known as one of the largest Black-owned properties in the United States at the time.

To this day, Greenwood is a powerful example of what can be achieved despite systemic oppression. Unfortunately, Greenwood would only enjoy its prosperity for about two decades before something terrible took place.

The Bloody Massacre

The infamous Tulsa Race Massacre occurred in 1921. It began with a false allegation involving a young African American shoe shiner named Dick Rowland. On May 30th, 1921, Rowland was said to have entered an elevator in Drexel Building. He was hoping to use the restroom on the topmost floor. Inside the elevator was also a White woman named Sarah Page. What happened in the elevator remains unclear. Some reported that Rowland either bumped into Page or accidentally stepped on her foot. Whatever happened, Rowland fled after the incident but was arrested the next day and accused of assault.

Although no one was able to confirm what happened during the incident (there were no witnesses), Rowland's name was smeared. Rumors of the alleged assault spread through Tulsa. Controversial headlines in local newspapers ignited racial tensions, which had been close to a boiling point.

A White mob gathered outside the courthouse where Rowland was being held. They demanded his lynching. This scene heightened the fear among the Black community. A group of armed Black men—most of them were veterans of World War I—made their way to the courthouse to protect Rowland from any harm. The Black community wanted to ensure that Rowland would receive a fair trial.

Suddenly, a gunshot was heard. No one knows who fired it, but it triggered a chain of violence. The White mob did not hesitate to wreak havoc. Knowing there was no turning back, the residents of Greenwood were left with no choice but to defend their homes and businesses that they had built for years. However, they were vastly outnumbered and outgunned.

Chaos overwhelmed the Black district on the night of May 31st, 1921. The White mobs had been given weapons by the local authorities, and they attacked the district. Homes were broken into and looted. Businesses were set ablaze with torches and incendiary weapons. The sky was not bright with stars; the night turned bright with flames. There were even airplanes (some said these were provided by local oil companies) dropping firebombs on Greenwood's homes and businesses.

The destruction continued until the morning of June 1st. Although Greenwood was already in a state of near-total destruction, thousands of White rioters charged into the district. They shot any resident on sight and burned everything in their path. Families fled for their lives. They desperately sought refuge where they could. The noises of daily life were replaced with the harrowing cries of the wounded and dying.

The state of Greenwood during the massacre.[33]

The massacre lasted for less than twenty-four hours, yet the destruction was immense. Black Wall Street was reduced to ashes. At least thirty-five blocks had either collapsed or burned down. Three hundred African American residents lay lifeless on the streets. This number, however, is only an estimate. It is impossible to confirm how many perished during the massacre. Only a few bodies were ever found. The rest were believed to have been buried in a mass grave; the exact location has yet to be discovered.

Those who survived were left with nothing. Despite this horrifying episode being named as one of the biggest racial massacres in history, none of the Whites involved were ever prosecuted or punished.

Greenwood after the massacre.[34]

Because of a small incident that was likely severely exaggerated, Greenwood suffered a massive economic disaster. Companies that had taken years to establish were ruined in a matter of hours.

Surviving families did not even have anything left to rebuild their houses and businesses. They turned to the insurance companies, but these insurance companies used riot exclusion clauses as justification for rejecting their claims. The community was in a state of mental torture. Not only were they grieving for the loss of their loved ones, but they also had to deal with the fear, anxiety, and despair caused by the violent and unjust destruction. These psychological scars would endure for generations.

Despite this terrible episode, the residents of Greenwood refused to give up. They worked together to rebuild their community. Churches, which had always been a source of encouragement, played a huge role in the recovery efforts. From the debris of the destruction, businesses reemerged.

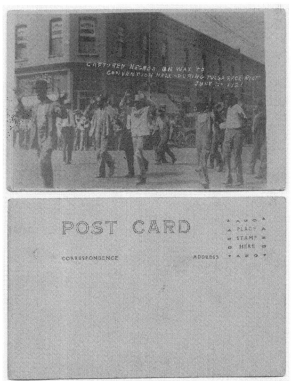

Postcards with images of the captured African Americans after the massacre, which acted as souvenirs for White collectors.[35]

While the community attempted to seek justice, the authorities turned a blind eye. The Tulsa Race Massacre was left out of official history books and public discourse for many years. It was not until the late 20th and early 21st centuries that the massacre was finally acknowledged.

Conclusion

As the pages of this book draw to a close, imagine the countless untold stories that have come to life within these chapters. Each narrative has revealed a unique facet of America's past, shedding light on events and individuals often overlooked by mainstream history.

Picture the ingenious Ghost Army of World War II, a secret unit whose creative deceptions misled enemy forces and altered the course of battles. Envision the enduring mystery of the lost colony of Roanoke, where an entire settlement vanished without a trace, leaving behind only questions and speculation. Reflect on the slave rebellions that shook the South, where courageous individuals rose up against their oppressors, challenging the brutal institution of slavery.

These stories are united by threads of courage, resilience, and innovation. They paint a broader, more inclusive picture of American history, highlighting the contributions of those who might otherwise remain in the shadows. By bringing these tales to light, a richer understanding of the past is achieved, one that honors the diversity of experiences and voices that have shaped the nation.

Let the curiosity sparked by these tales inspire further exploration. Seek out stories that challenge conventional narratives and broaden the scope of understanding. History is not a static record but an evolving dialogue, inviting continuous discovery and reinterpretation. By delving into the hidden facets of the past, new insights emerge, offering a more nuanced perspective on the present.

Countless stories await to be discovered, each adding another layer to the intricate portrait of America's past. Let this book be the beginning of your journey to explore the many dimensions of history that continue to shape our world.

If you enjoyed this book, I'd greatly appreciate a review on Amazon because it helps me to create more books that people want. It would mean a lot to hear from you.

To leave a review:

1. Open your camera app.
2. Point your mobile device at the QR code.
3. The review page will appear in your web browser.

Thanks for your support!

Here's another book by Matt Clayton that you might like

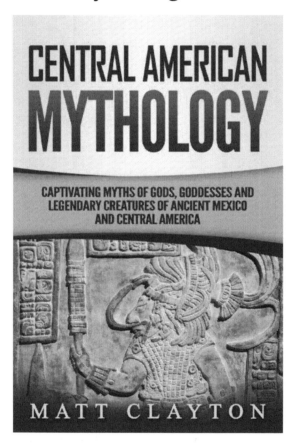

Bibliography

Alexander, Kathy. "Pearl Hart – Lady Bandit of Arizona." Legends of America, n.d. https://www.legendsofamerica.com/we-pearlhart/.

Andrews, Evan. "7 Things You May Not Know About Geronimo." History, April 3, 2024. https://www.history.com/news/7-things-you-may-not-know-about-geronimo.

Boessenecker, J. "The True Story of Pearl Hart, Straight-Shooting, Poetry-Writing Woman Bandit," Literary Hub. November 11, 2021. https://lithub.com/the-true-story-of-pearl-hart-straight-shooting-poetry-writing-woman-bandit/.

Carlton, Genevieve. "Meet Josephine Earp, the Mysterious Wife of Wyatt Earp." All That's Interesting, December 11, 2021. https://allthatsinteresting.com/josephine-earp.

Carr, E. Patrick. "Norton I, Emperor of the United States," n.d. https://www.molossia.org/norton.html.

DeCosta-Klipa, Nik. "It's Been Exactly 98 Years Since a Giant Wave of Molasses Killed 21 People in Boston." Boston.com, January 17, 2017. https://www.boston.com/news/history/2017/01/15/its-been-exactly-98-years-since-a-giant-wave-of-molasses-killed-21-people-in-boston/.

"Eleanore Dumont – Madame Mustache Plays to the West," Legends of America, n.d. https://www.legendsofamerica.com/we-eleanoredumont/.

"Emperor Norton: Life & Legend," The Emperor Norton Trust, n.d. https://emperornortontrust.org/emperor/life.

Gara, Antoine. "The Baron of Black Wall Street." Forbes, May 31, 2021. https://www.forbes.com/sites/antoinegara/2020/06/18/the-bezos-of-black-wall-street-tulsa-race-riots-1921/.

"Geronimo," Biography, February 22, 2024.
https://www.biography.com/political-figures/geronimo.

Hewitt, Les. "Hellfire Club History: Beginnings of the Infamous Secret
Society." Historic Mysteries, September 16, 2020.
https://www.historicmysteries.com/history/hellfire-club/4225/.

"Jermain Wesley Loguen," National Underground Railroad Freedom Center,
n.d. https://freedomcenter.org/heroes/jermain-wesley-loguen/.

Johns, Kieren. "Spartacus: What Is the True Story of the Slave Who Led a
Rebellion?" TheCollector, September 14, 2023.
https://www.thecollector.com/spartacus-gladiator/.

"Laura Smith Haviland," National Abolition Hall Of Fame And Museum. n.d.
https://www.nationalabolitionhalloffameandmuseum.org/laura-smith-
haviland.html.

Levi, Ryan. "America's Emperor, San Francisco's Treasure: Who Was
Emperor Norton?" KQED, November 21, 2023.
https://www.kqed.org/news/11652705/americas-emperor-san-franciscos-
treasure-who-was-emperor-norton.

Melton, J. Gordon. "Rosicrucian | Definition, History, & Facts." Encyclopedia
Britannica, July 20, 1998. https://www.britannica.com/topic/Rosicrucians.

Milligan, Mark. "The Secret Hellfire Club." HeritageDaily, November 2, 2021.
https://www.heritagedaily.com/2020/08/the-secret-hellfire-club-and-the-hellfire-
caves/134801.

Onion, Rebecca. "Postcards Celebrating the Ruins of Black Neighborhoods
After the Tulsa Race Riot of 1921." Slate Magazine, July 29, 2014.
https://slate.com/human-interest/2014/07/tulsa-race-riot-history-postcards-
made-with-images-of-ruins-of-black-communities.html.

"Operation Brest | the Ghost Army Legacy Project," n.d.
https://ghostarmy.org/about/operation-
brest/#:~:text=August%2020%2D27%2C%201944&text=Operation%20BREST
%20marked%20the%20first,midst%20of%20a%20major%20battle.

Powers, Thomas. "How The Battle of Little Bighorn Was Won." Smithsonian
Magazine, November 17, 2013. https://www.smithsonianmag.com/history/how-
the-battle-of-little-bighorn-was-won-63880188/.

Schiavino, G.R. "The Notorious Pearl Hart." American Cowboy, June 14,
2023. https://americancowboy.com/people/pearl-hart-female-outlaw-yuma-
territorial-prison/.

Significance, Battle of the Little Bighorn - Location Cause &. "Battle of the
Little Bighorn - Location, Cause & Significance." History, December 21, 2020.
https://www.history.com/topics/native-american-history/battle-of-the-little-
bighorn.

"Sir Francis Dashwood," Chilterns National Landscape, July 13, 2022. https://www.chilterns.org.uk/map_marker/sir-francis-dashwood/.

"Society of the Cincinnati," George Washington's Mount Vernon, n.d. https://www.mountvernon.org/library/digitalhistory/digital-encyclopedia/article/society-of-the-cincinnati.

Sohn, Emily. "Why The Great Molasses Flood Was so Deadly." History, August 4, 2023. https://www.history.com/news/great-molasses-flood-science.

Stables, Dan. "The Original Hellfire Club: Where British Elites Practiced Pagan Rites and Bacchanalian Orgies." Fodors Travel Guide, September 27, 2022. https://www.fodors.com/world/europe/england/experiences/news/whats-the-hellfire-club-the-secret-society-of-british-elites-who-performed-pagan-rites.

Stengle, Jamie. "Ghost Army Members Who Deceived Nazis With Battlefield Ruses in WWII Given Congressional Gold Medal." AP News, March 21, 2024. https://apnews.com/article/ghost-army-congressional-gold-medal-ceremony-world-war-ii-7a2deaf1686bca3194d46c77fa0bccb9.

Waxman, Olivia B. "The Most Important Slave Revolt That Never Happened." Time, March 15, 2017. https://time.com/4701283/denmark-vesey-history-charleston-south-carolina/.

Image Sources

[1] *Rolf Müller, CC BY-SA 3.0 <http://creativecommons.org/licenses/by-sa/3.0/>, via Wikimedia Commons: https://commons.wikimedia.org/wiki/File:Mount_gulian_fishkill_closeup_2006.jpg*

[2] *Daderot, CC0, via Wikimedia Commons: https://commons.wikimedia.org/wiki/File:Badge_of_the_Society_of_the_Cincinnati,_c._1783,_gold_and_enamel_-_Cincinnati_Art_Museum_-_DSC04560.JPG*

[3] *Andrew Smith / Medmenham Abbey: https://commons.wikimedia.org/wiki/File:Medmenham_Abbey_-_geograph.org.uk_-_762469.jpg*

[4] *Neil Rickards from London, England, CC BY 2.0 <https://creativecommons.org/licenses/by/2.0>, via Wikimedia Commons: https://commons.wikimedia.org/wiki/File:Hellfire_Caves_tunnel.jpg*

[5] *https://commons.wikimedia.org/wiki/File:Slaveshipposter.jpg*

[6] *Jud McCranie, CC BY-SA 4.0 <https://creativecommons.org/licenses/by-sa/4.0>, via Wikimedia Commons: https://commons.wikimedia.org/wiki/File:Igbo_Landing_area,_Glynn_County,_Georgia,_US.jpg*

[7] *https://commons.wikimedia.org/wiki/File:The_Englishmen%27s_arrival_in_Virginia_(1590).jpg*

[8] *https://commons.wikimedia.org/wiki/File:A_popular_history_of_the_United_States_-_from_the_first_discovery_of_the_western_hemisphere_by_the_Northmen,_to_the_end_of_the_first_century_of_the_union_of_the_states;_preceded_by_a_sketch_of_the_(14781233224).jpg*

[9] *Nesnad, CC BY 4.0 <https://creativecommons.org/licenses/by/4.0>, via Wikimedia Commons: https://commons.wikimedia.org/wiki/File:Darestone.svg*

[10] *https://commons.wikimedia.org/wiki/File:Undergroundrailroadsmall2.jpg*

[11] *https://commons.wikimedia.org/wiki/File:LauraSmithHaviland1910.png*

[12] *https://commons.wikimedia.org/wiki/File:Jermain_Wesley_Loguen_(engraving).png*

[13] https://commons.wikimedia.org/wiki/File:John_P._Parker_House_from_northwest.jpg

[14] https://commons.wikimedia.org/wiki/File:DummyShermanTank.jpg

[15] https://commons.wikimedia.org/wiki/File:Ghost_Army_Medal.jpg

[16] https://commons.wikimedia.org/wiki/File:Nort10d.jpg

[17] https://commons.wikimedia.org/wiki/File:Emperor_Joshua_A._Norton_I.jpg

[18] https://commons.wikimedia.org/wiki/File:The_Cow_Boy_1888.jpg

[19] https://commons.wikimedia.org/wiki/File:PearlHart.jpg

[20] https://commons.wikimedia.org/wiki/File:Annie_Oakley_by_Baker%27s_Art_Gallery_c1880s-crop.jpg

[21] https://commons.wikimedia.org/wiki/File:Pearl_Hart_in_Jail_Cell.jpg

[22] https://commons.wikimedia.org/wiki/File:Eleanore_dumont.jpg

[23] https://commons.wikimedia.org/wiki/File:Josephine_Sarah_Marcus_1880.png

[24] https://commons.wikimedia.org/wiki/File:Wyatt_and_Josephine_Earp_1906.jpg

[25] https://commons.wikimedia.org/wiki/File:North_End_molasses_tank.jpg

[26] https://commons.wikimedia.org/wiki/File:BostonMolassesDisaster.jpg

[27] https://commons.wikimedia.org/wiki/File:Boston_1919_molasses_disaster_-_el_train_structure.jpg

[28] https://commons.wikimedia.org/wiki/File:Charles_Marion_Russell_-_The_Custer_Fight_(1903).jpg

[29] https://commons.wikimedia.org/wiki/File:Little_Big_Horn.jpg

[30] https://commons.wikimedia.org/wiki/File:Apache_chief_Geronimo_(right)_and_his_warriors_in_1886.jpg

[31] https://commons.wikimedia.org/wiki/File:Geronimo%27s_grave_taken_in_2005.jpg

[32] https://commons.wikimedia.org/wiki/File:JimCrowInDurhamNC.jpg

[33] https://commons.wikimedia.org/wiki/File:TulsaRaceRiot-1921.png

[34] https://commons.wikimedia.org/wiki/File:Tulsa_Aftermath.jpg

[35] https://commons.wikimedia.org/wiki/File:Captured_Negros_on_Way_to_Convention_Hall_-_During_Tulsa_Race_Riot,_June_1st,_1921_(14412915233).jpg

Made in the USA
Middletown, DE
14 November 2024

64566146R00062